# Colour Me
# WILD

First Published in the UK in 2016 by
Apple Press
74-77 White Lion Street
London N1 9PF
UK
www.apple-press.com

10 9 8 7 6 5 4 3 2

Manufactured in China

ISBN: 978-1-8454-3657-5

Publisher: Mark Searle
Editorial Director: Isheeta Mustafi
Commissioning Editor: Alison Morris
Junior Editor: Abbie Sharman
Editor: Joanne Reeder
Cover design: Michelle Rowlandson
Layout: Michelle Rowlandson and Agata Rybicka

# TRIANIMALS

# Colour Me
# WILD

## 60 Colour-by-Number
## Geometric Artworks with Bite

HOPE LITTLE & ÇETIN CAN KARADUMAN

APPLEPRESS

# Welcome to
# TRIANIMALS

Raccoon

18

Yak

19

Iguana

20

Red Panda

21

Lemur

22

Peacock

23

Crested Crane

24

Slow Loris

25

Poison Dart Frog

26

Stag

28

Meerkat

29

Mountain Goat

30

Gorilla

31

Capybara

32

Armadillo

33

Giraffe

34

Hedgehog

35

Anteater

36

Aye-aye

38

Platypus

39

Common Seal

40

Chameleon

41

Sloth

42

Hare

43

Penguin
44

Hippopotamus
45

Bobcat
46

Otter
48

Cheetah
49

Tortoise
50

Opossum
51

Brown Bear
52

Golden Lion Tamarin
53

Hyena
54

Mandrill
55

Koala
56

Alligator
58

Fox
59

Llama
60

Camel
61

Badger
62

Beaver
63

Elephant
64

Kangaroo
65

Red Squirrel
66

Panda
68

Wolf
69

Lioness
70

Wombat
71

Wild Boar
72

Okapi
73

Cape Buffalo
74

MASKS

Zebra
81

Orangutan
83

Tiger
85

Vampire Bat
87

Lion
89

Great Horned Owl
91

Leopard
93

Chimpanzee
95

# LET'S GET WILD!

Welcome to the wonderful world of *Trianimals*. In this book you will find a whole menagerie of wild animals that have been illustrated using hundreds of triangles of varying sizes. Whether it's a red panda, mountain goat, chameleon, meerkat, buffalo or penguin, it's time to choose your favourite animal and get colouring.

The colours used in the palettes are as close to the real thing as possible, meaning that these exciting creatures come to life on every page. Each animal in the book has very different facial features, attitudes, patterns, colour combinations and characteristics – carefully colour in the images and watch as the animals start to reveal themselves, leaping out of the pages in glorious technicolour.

Colouring is the perfect pastime, aiding relaxation and allowing you to focus all your energy on a calm, quiet activity. So lose yourself in the pages of this book and discover talents you never knew you had. You can also join us online! Share your coloured-in animal on social media using the hashtag #Trianimals.

## FROM THE AUTHORS

When thinking about creating this book, we found inspiration in many areas: the natural world, photographs found online and also computer graphics. We wanted to experiment, test our capabilities, and this book is the result. Why triangles? It's the shape that offers the most variety, they work very well together and enable us to create complex images of each animal's head by using different sizes and combinations.

We have always loved wild animals so were naturally drawn to using them as our subject matter. They are all so different, with unique characteristics, colours and personalities. We hope you enjoy colouring them as much as we enjoyed creating them.

## MATERIALS

Invest in a pack of coloured pencils or felt-tip pens, and try to replicate the lightness and darkness of each shade. It's the light and dark triangles sitting side by side that give the images their depth and amazing 3-D look.

If you don't have coloured pencils or felt-tip pens, you could try watercolours or paint, and mix your own colours to create the right shade. But stay away from pastels as these are quite thick and it will be difficult to fill in the smaller triangles. Avoid charcoal too as this is likely to smudge, ruining all your hard work.

## TECHNIQUES

Stay inside the lines and keep your pencils sharp so you have maximum control in the smaller areas. Sharpen your pencils frequently to achieve crisp, clean images.

If the colour of your pencil doesn't quite match our colour palette, try blending, cross-hatching and adding more layers until you get the colour you want. Take your time – a masterpiece was never created in a day!

If you are struggling to create a particular shade, try substituting that colour for one you have available, or you could create your own colour palette, just remember to keep dark shades dark and light shades light.

To achieve a darker shade, try layering the colour until you get the right shade. Pressing harder with your coloured pencil should also achieve this result.

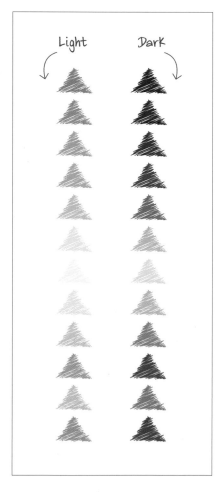

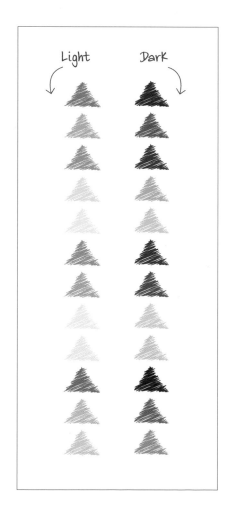

## USING THE COLOUR PALETTE

Two colour palettes have been created alongside the illustrations in this book. The natural palette is based on the animal's natural colouring and the vivid palette can be used to create a more vibrant and graphic look.

### NO NUMBER?

On the main illustration, if a triangle doesn't have a number that area is white, so there is no need to colour it in.

### USING THE NATURAL PALETTE

The key to getting your animals to look like the original image is to follow the natural palette as closely as possible.

### USING THE VIVID PALETTE

If you're looking for something a bit brighter, or just a bit different, try our vivid colour palettes.

### FREESTYLING

Avid colourers will spot that there are no colour palettes on the patterned pages for the poison dart frog, koala or red squirrel. There are also 'colour me in' versions of the openers for each section. These animals have been left unnumbered so you can let your imagination run wild.

This is your chance to experiment with different colours and techniques. Why not create your own colour palette around your favourite colour, or create a wacky pattern using a pop art style?

For the best results, think about your shading. Imagine where the sun would catch the animal in real life and try to keep those areas lighter than areas in the shade. The diagrams on page 12 show how the same colour can be used in different ways to achieve this.

Look out for the animal's natural colour palette at the top of each design.

NATURAL 1 2 3 4 5

Red Panda

VIVID 1 2 3 4 5

Are you ready to experiment? Try the vivid colour palette at the bottom of the page.

# Raccoon

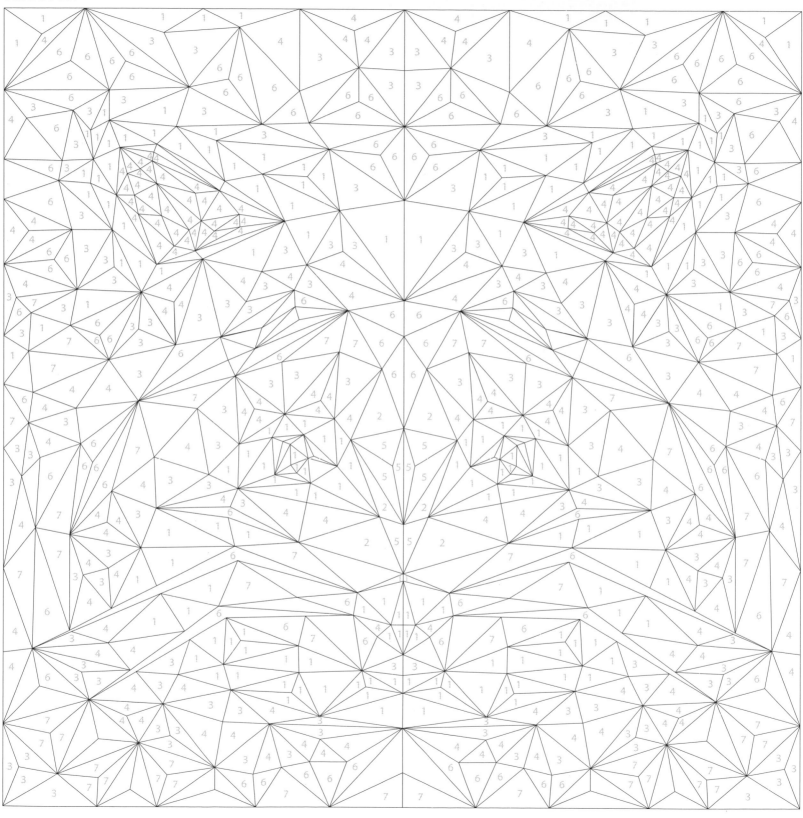

Yak

Iguana

1  2  3  4  5  6  7  8

Red Panda

1  2  3  4  5  6  7  8

# Lemur

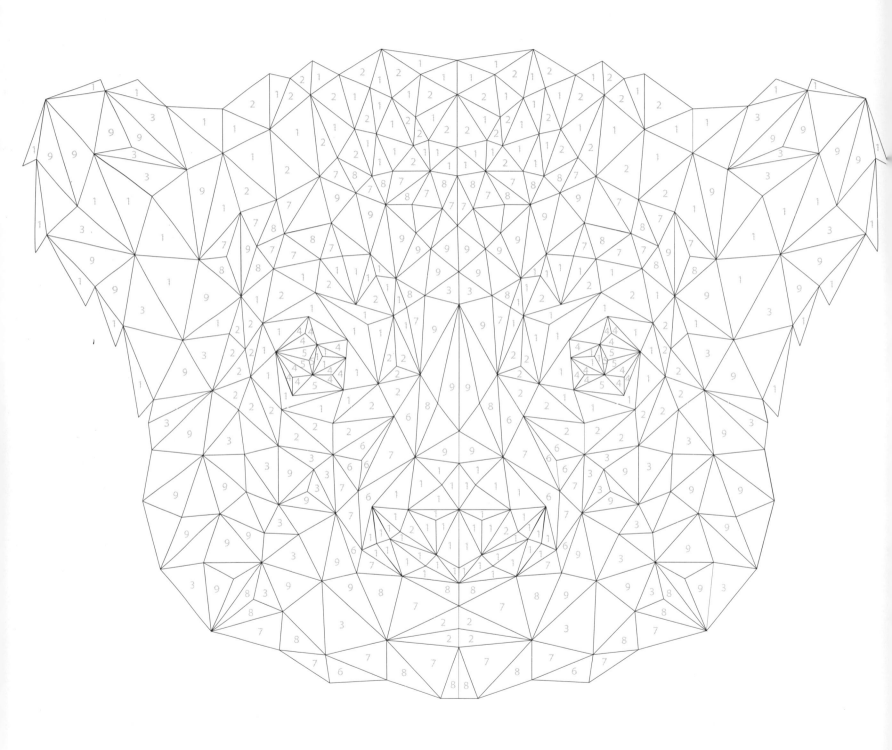

# Crested Crane

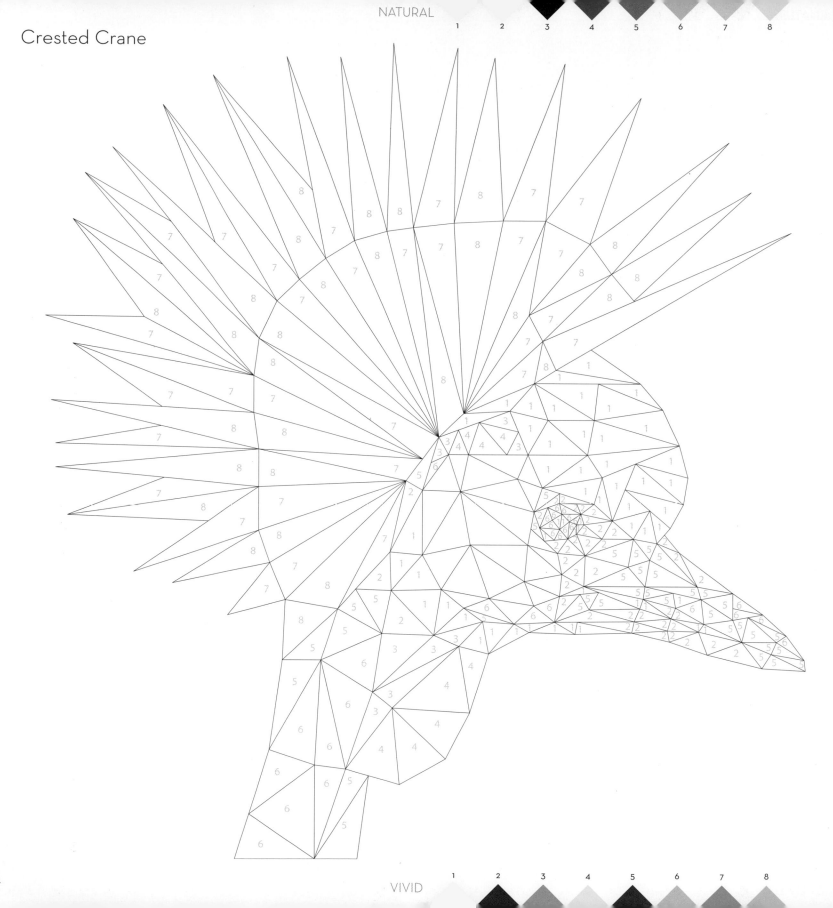

Slow Loris

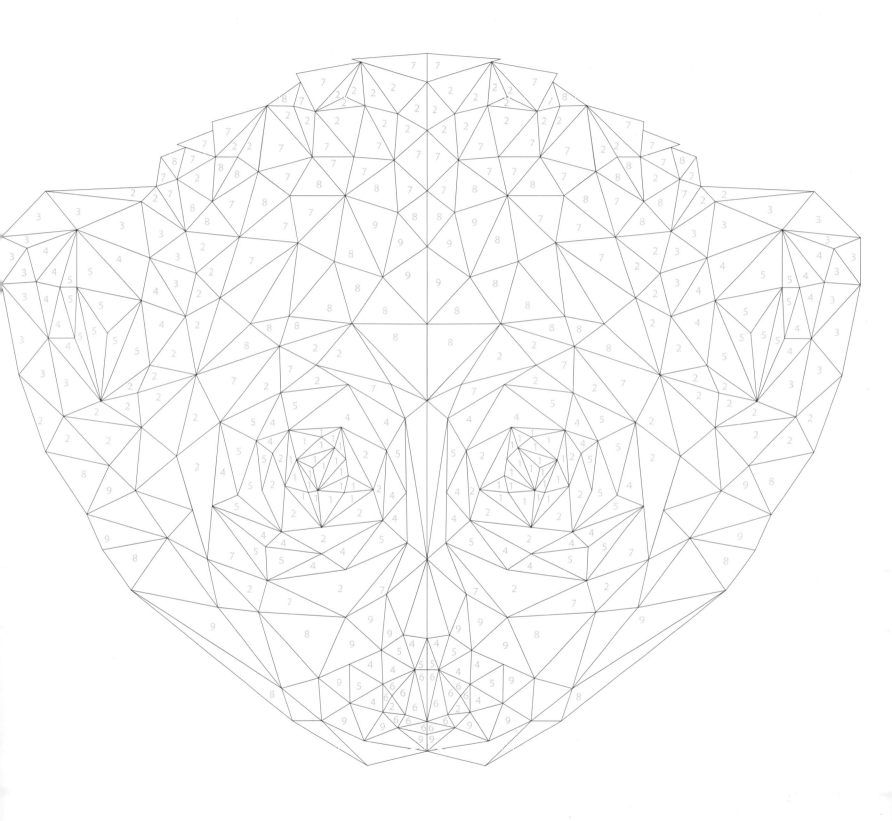

# Poison Dart Frog

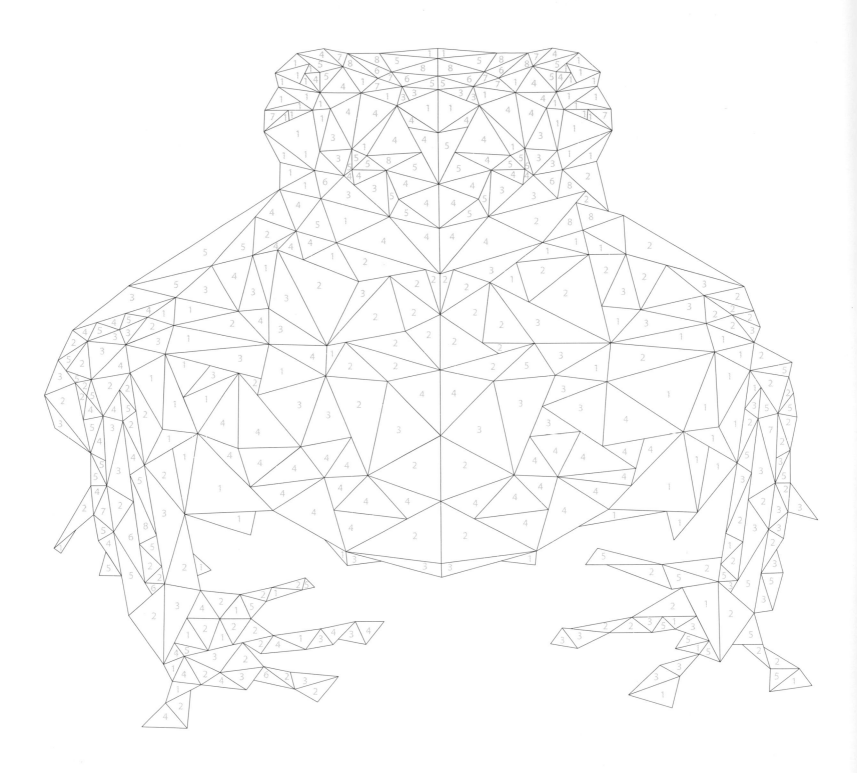

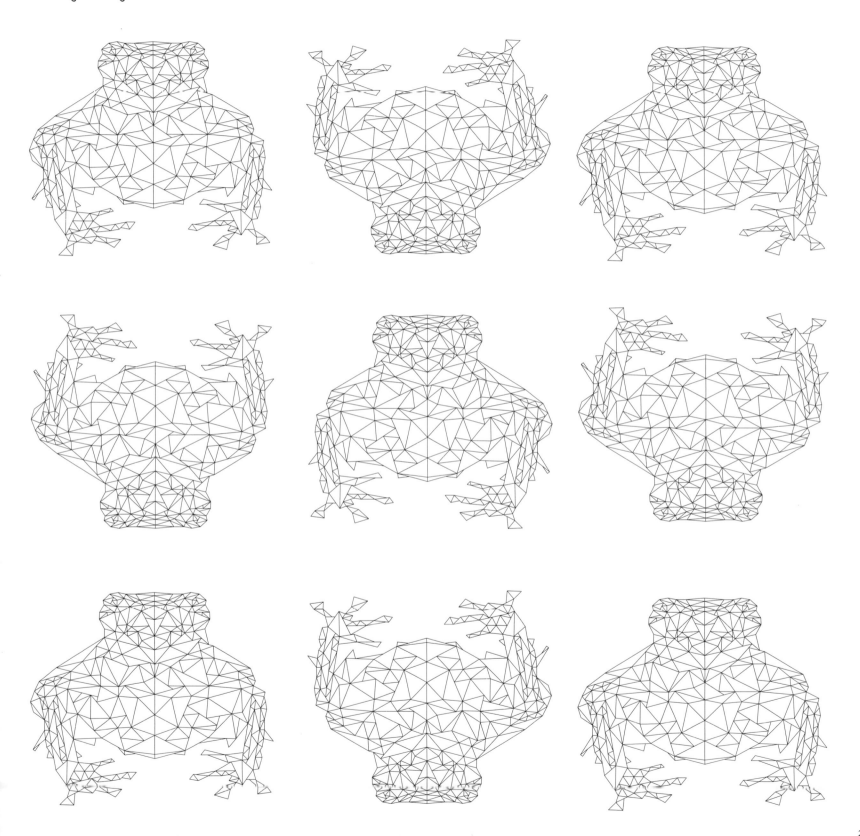

# Stag

Meerkat

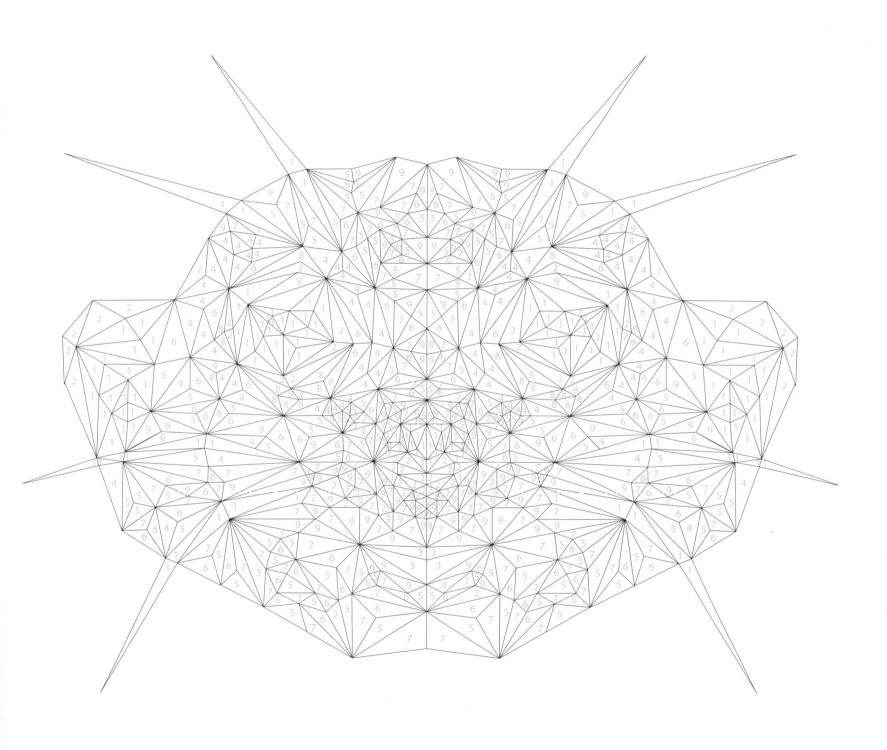

# Mountain Goat

VIVID

Gorilla

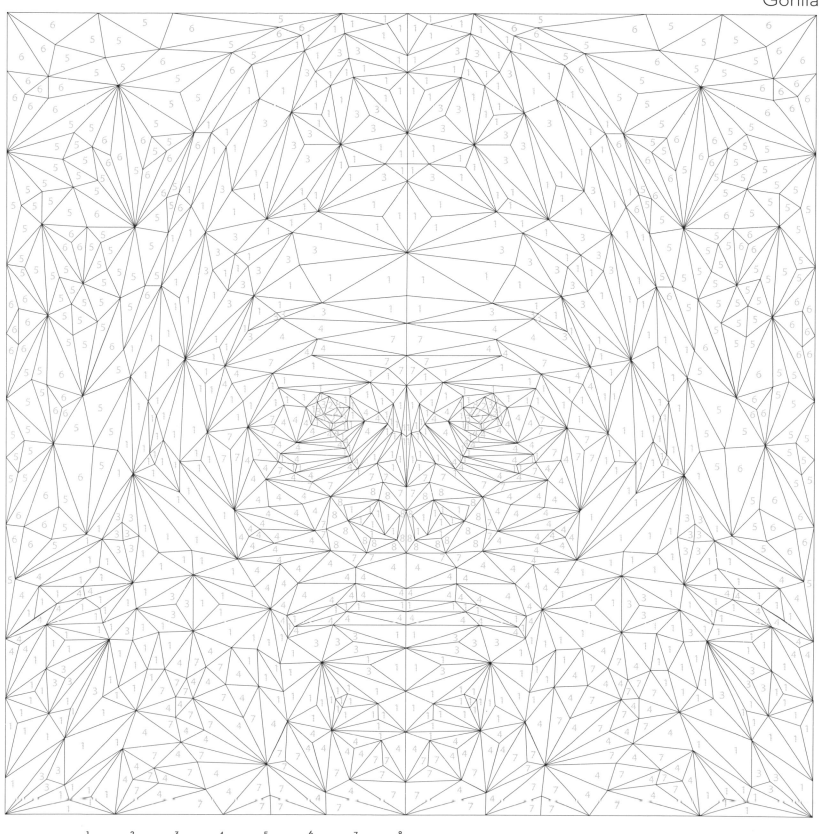

# Capybara

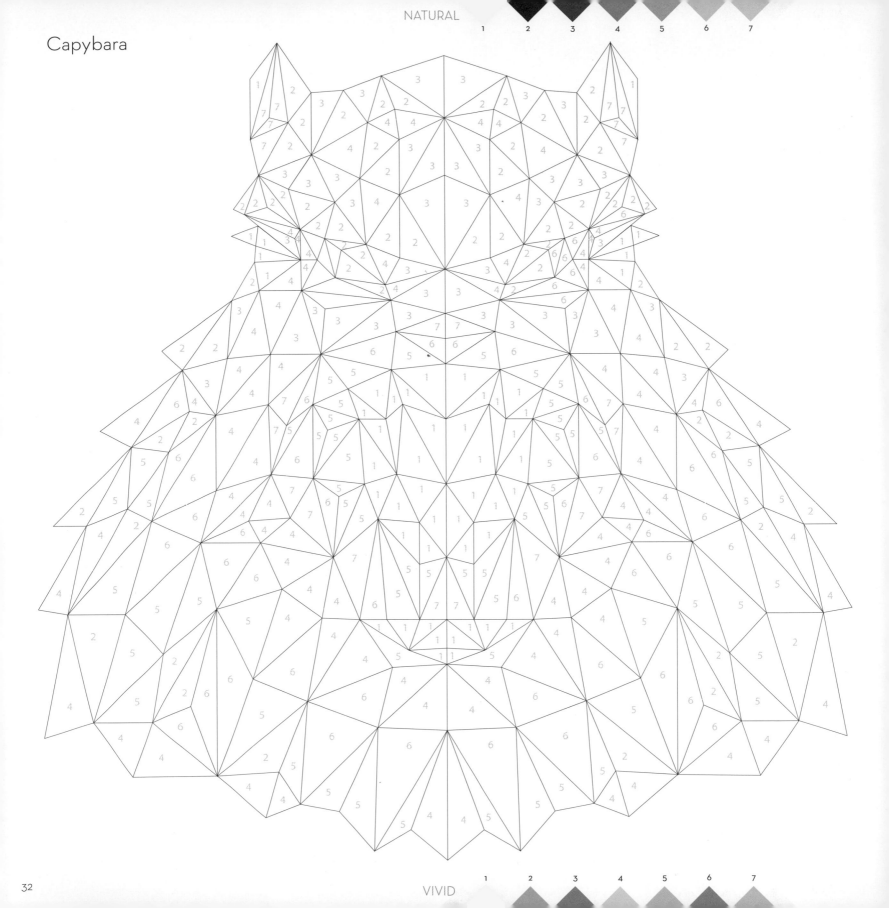

Armadillo

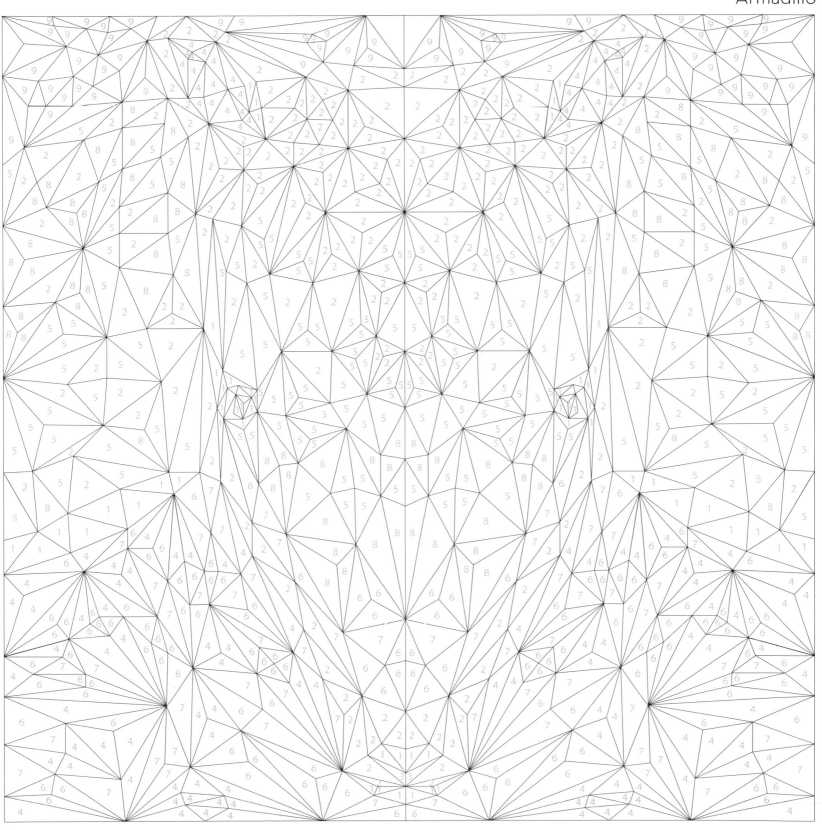

# Giraffe

1 2 3 4 5 6 7 8

# Hedgehog

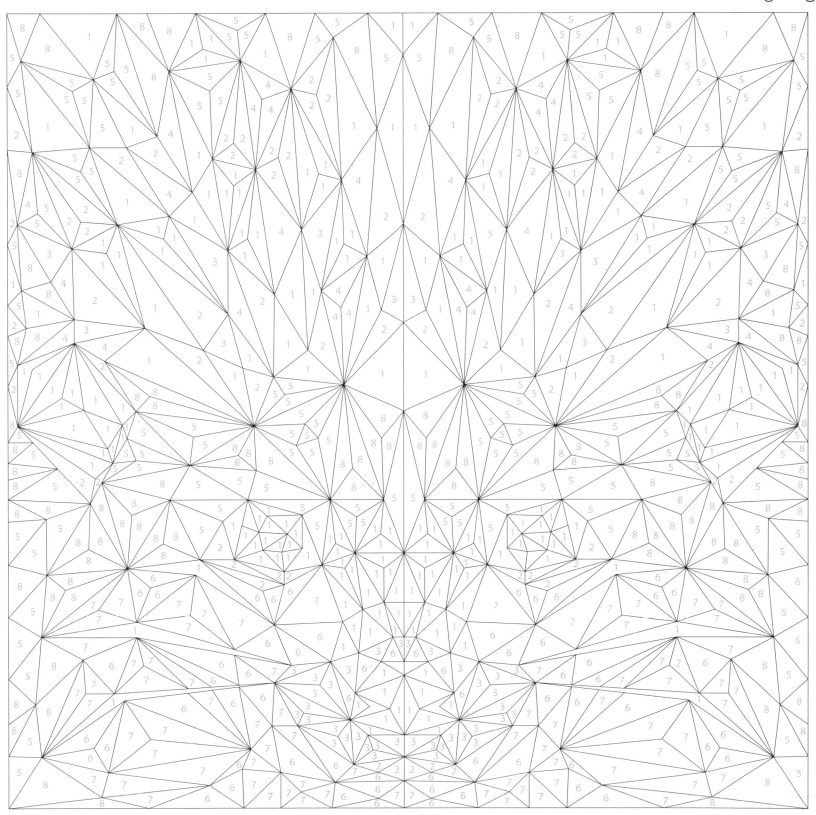

# Anteater

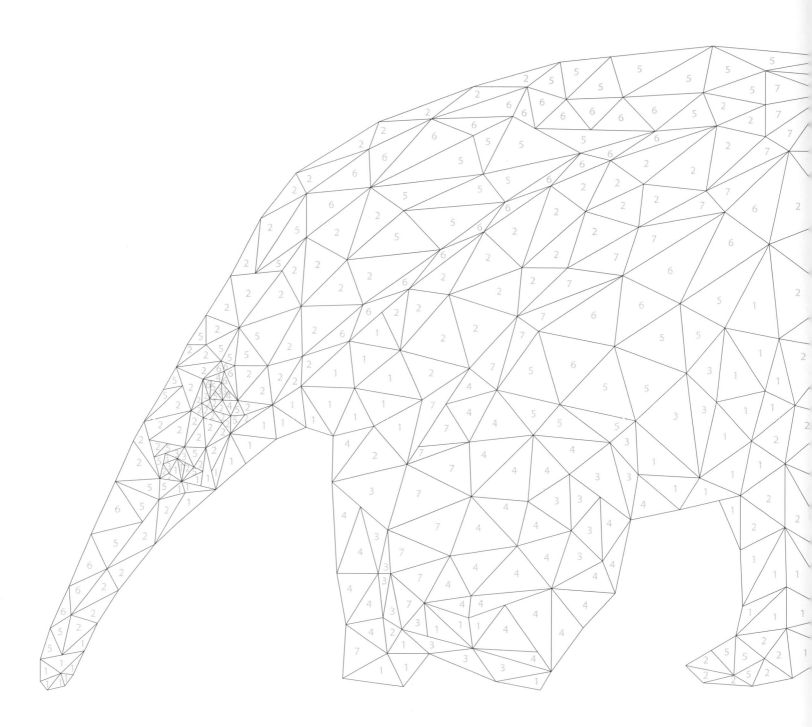

1  2  3  4  5  6  7

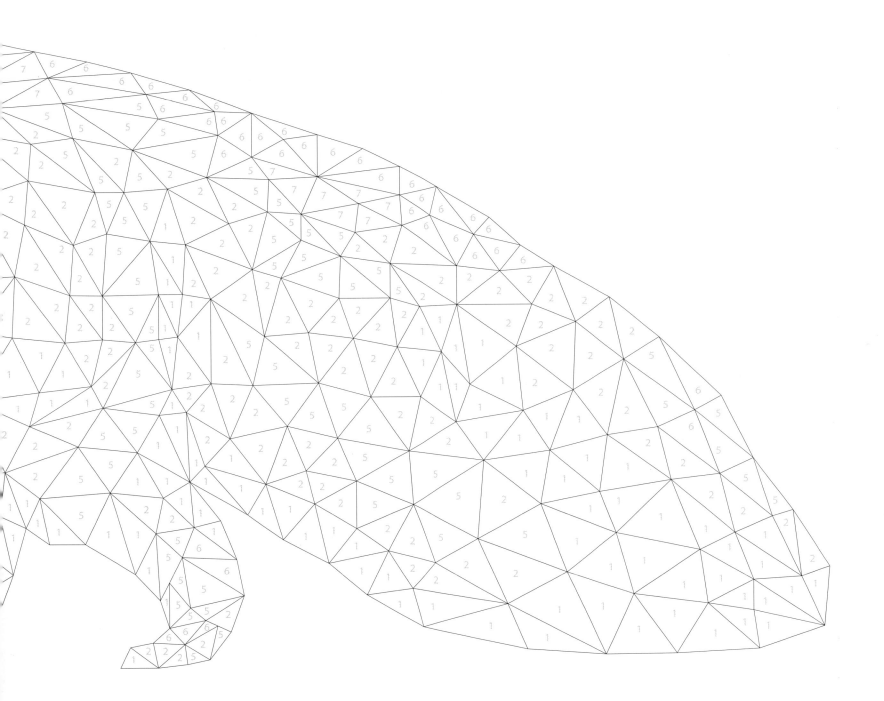

# Aye-aye

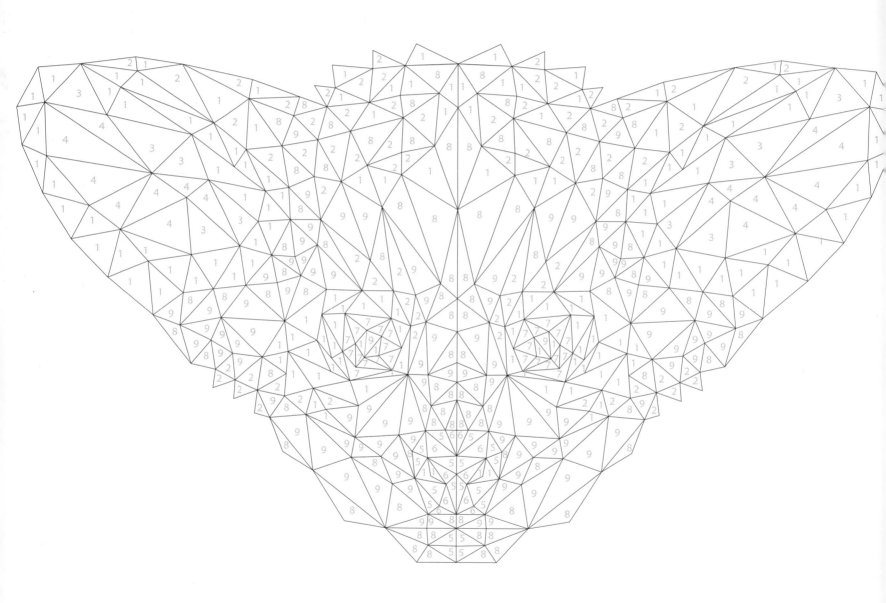

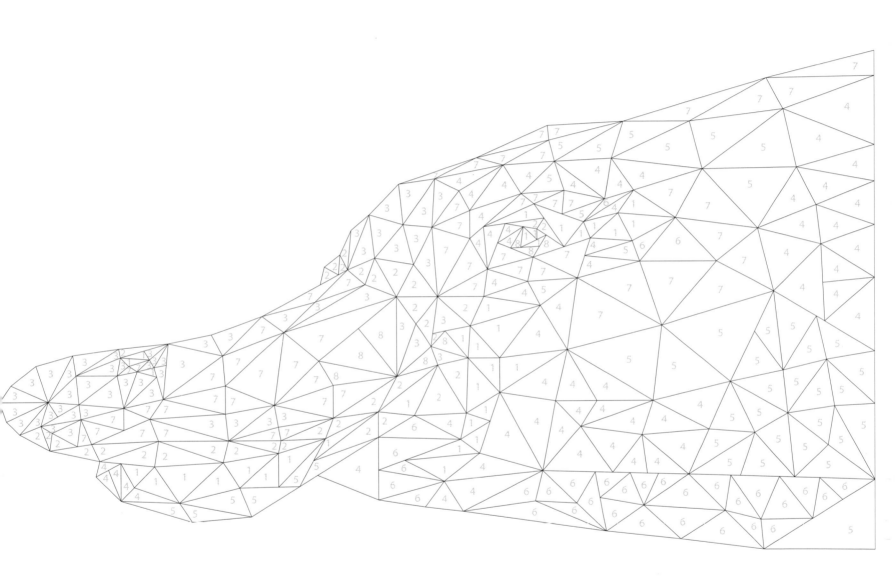

# Common Seal

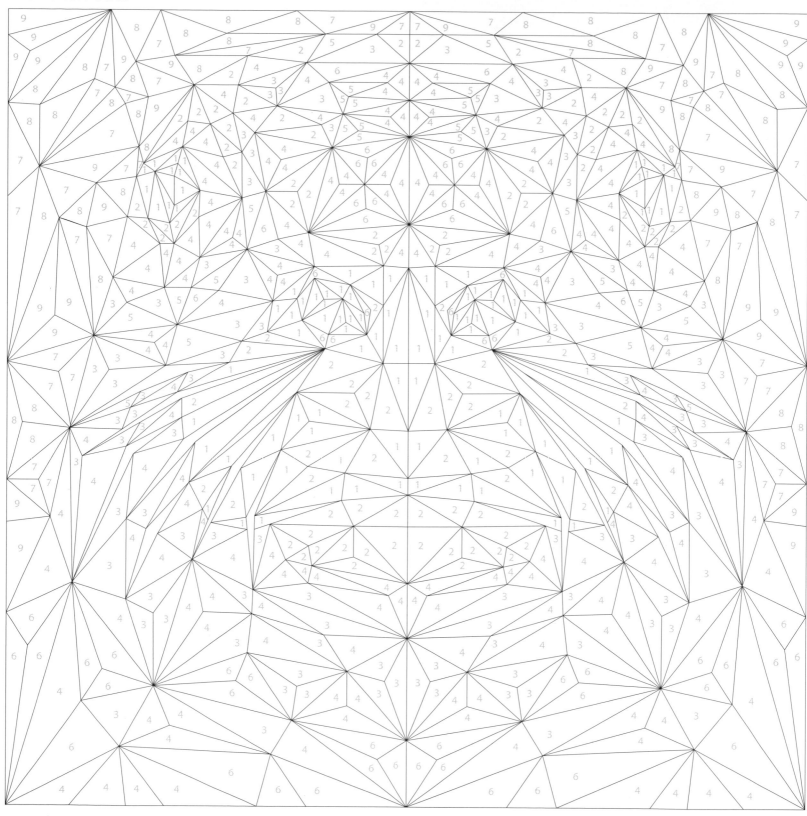

Chameleon

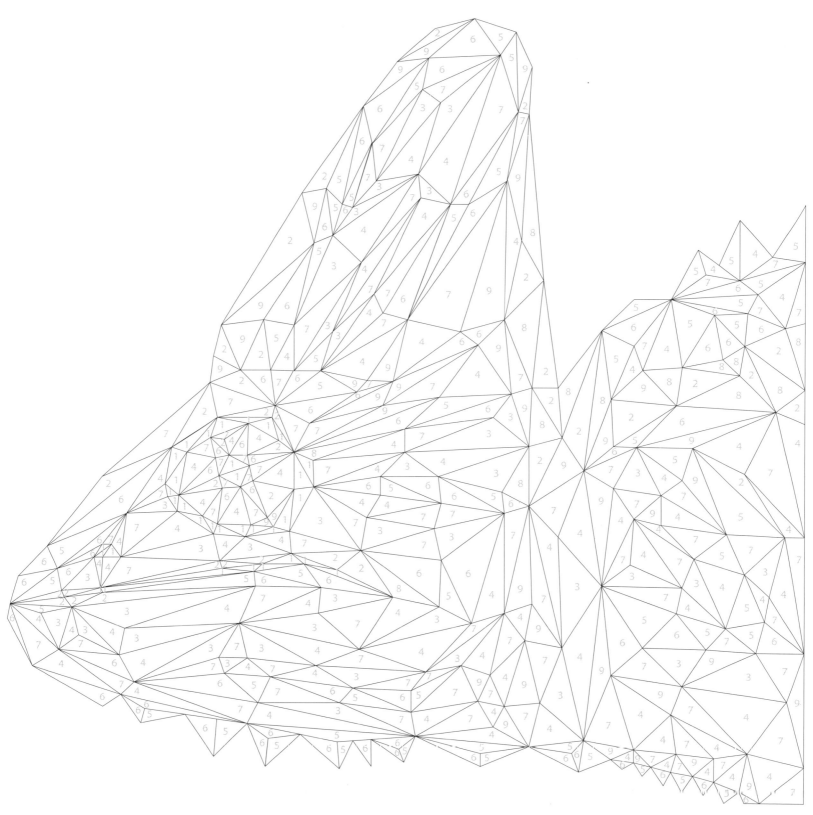

# Sloth

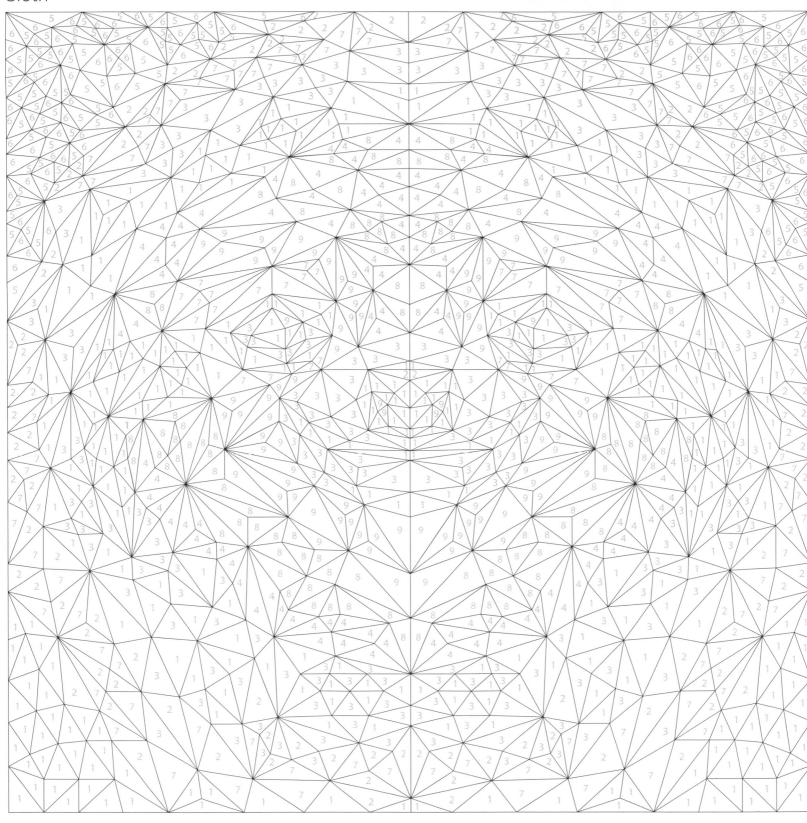

1 2 3 4 5 6 7 8 9

Hare

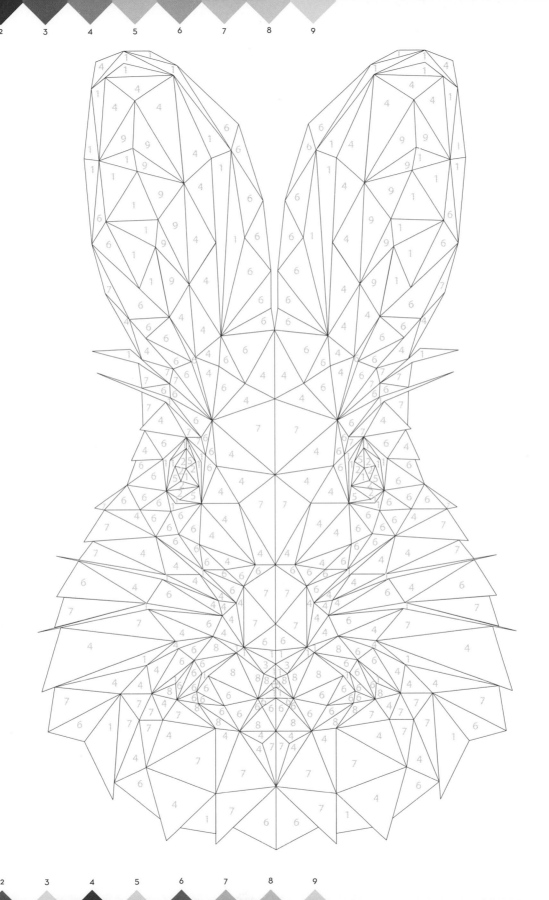

# Penguin

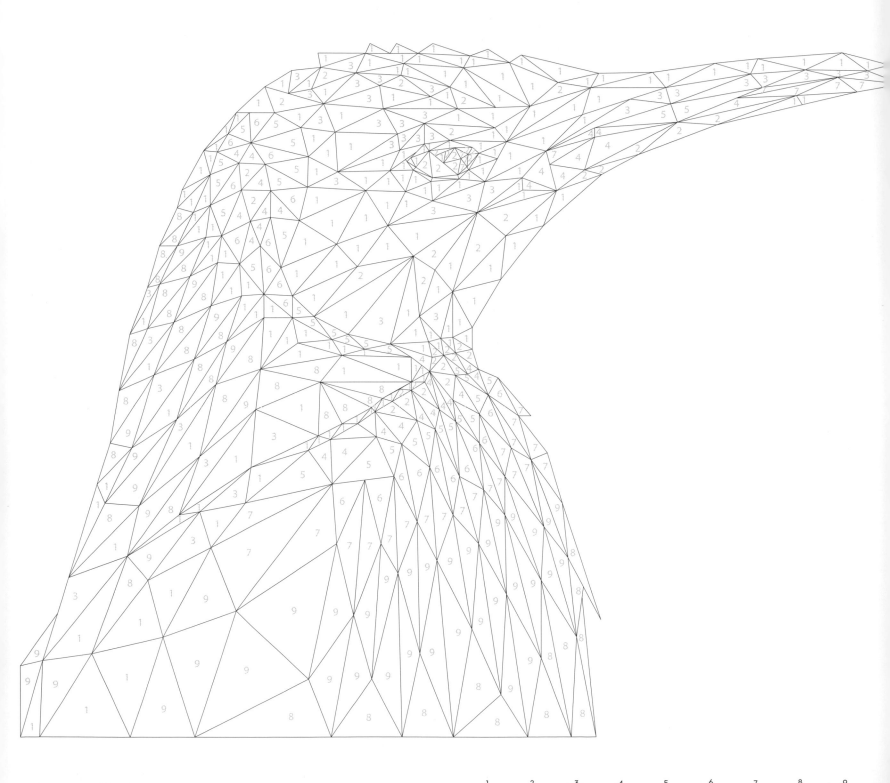

Hippopotamus

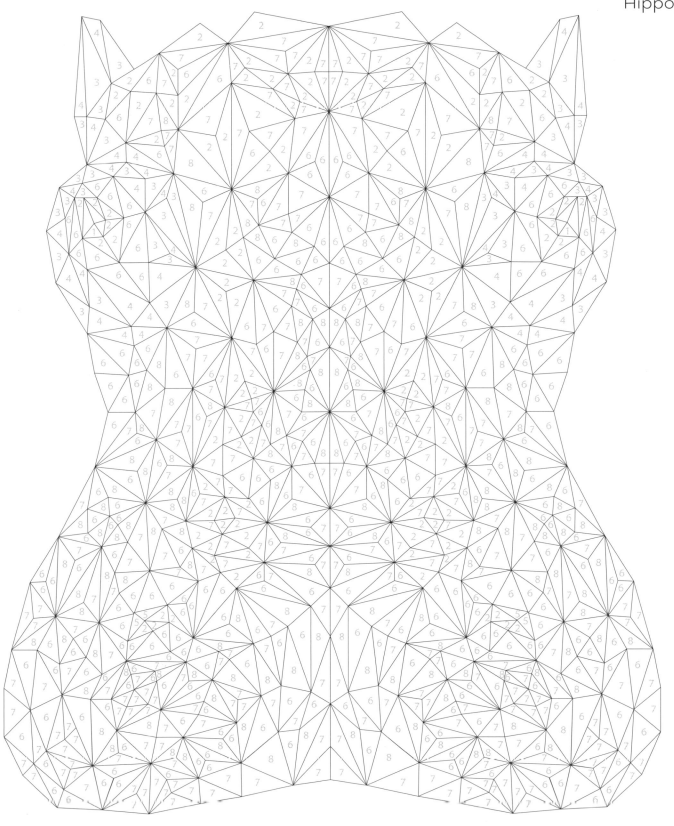

# Bobcat

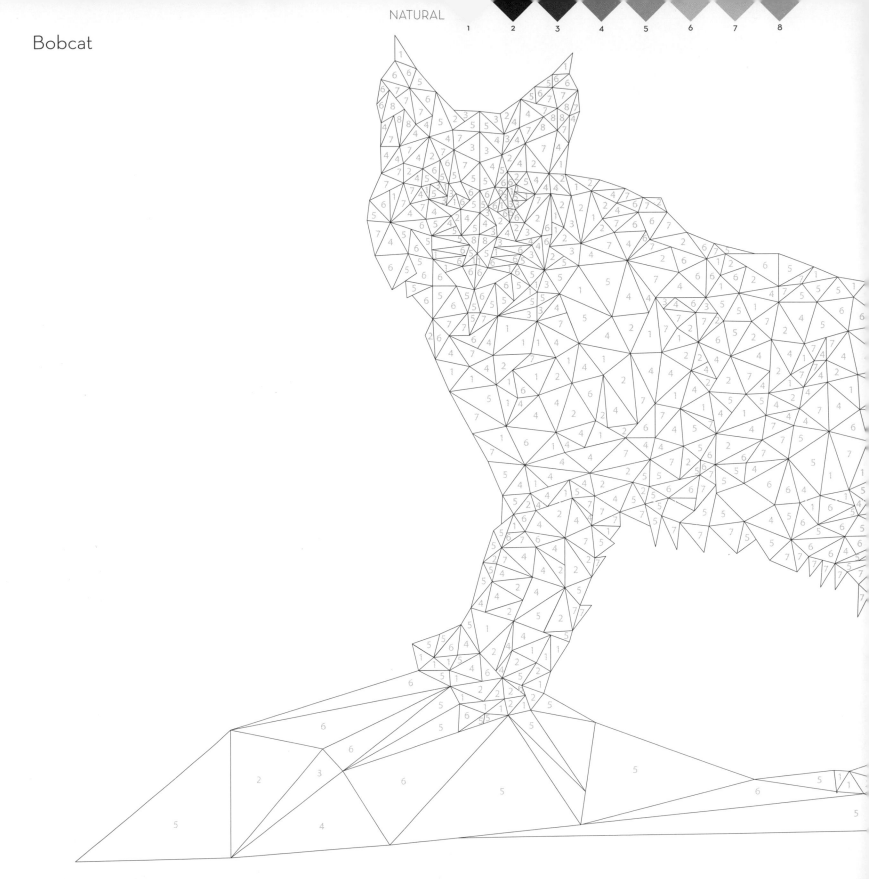

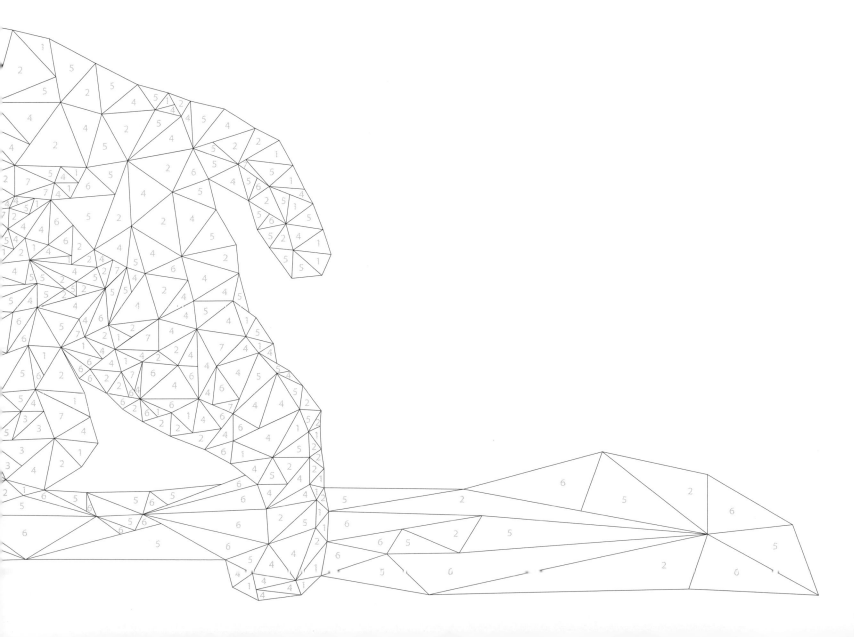

# Otter

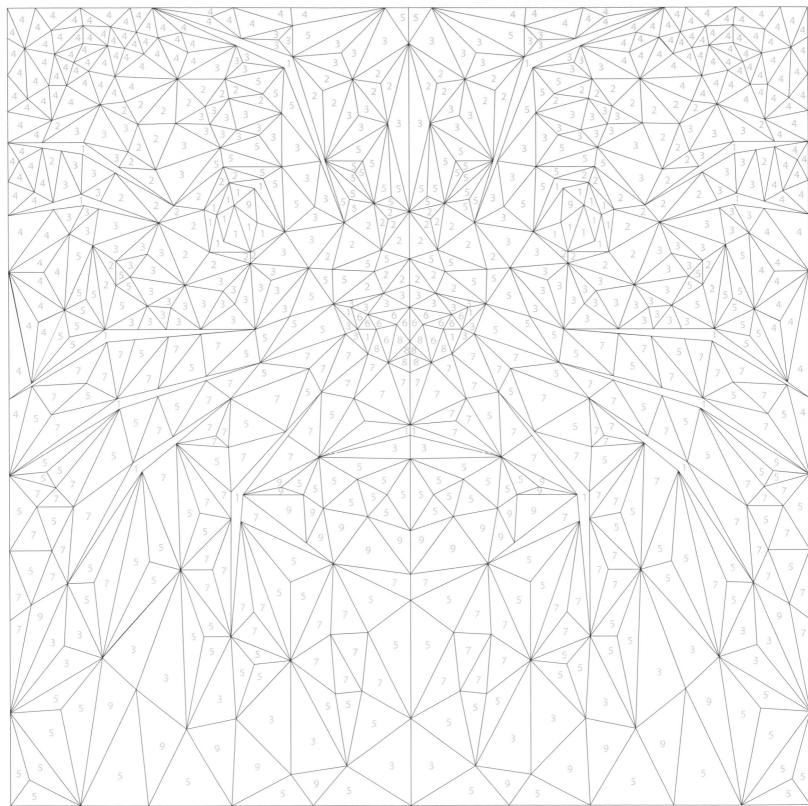

NATURAL

1 2 3 4 5 6 7 8 9

# Cheetah

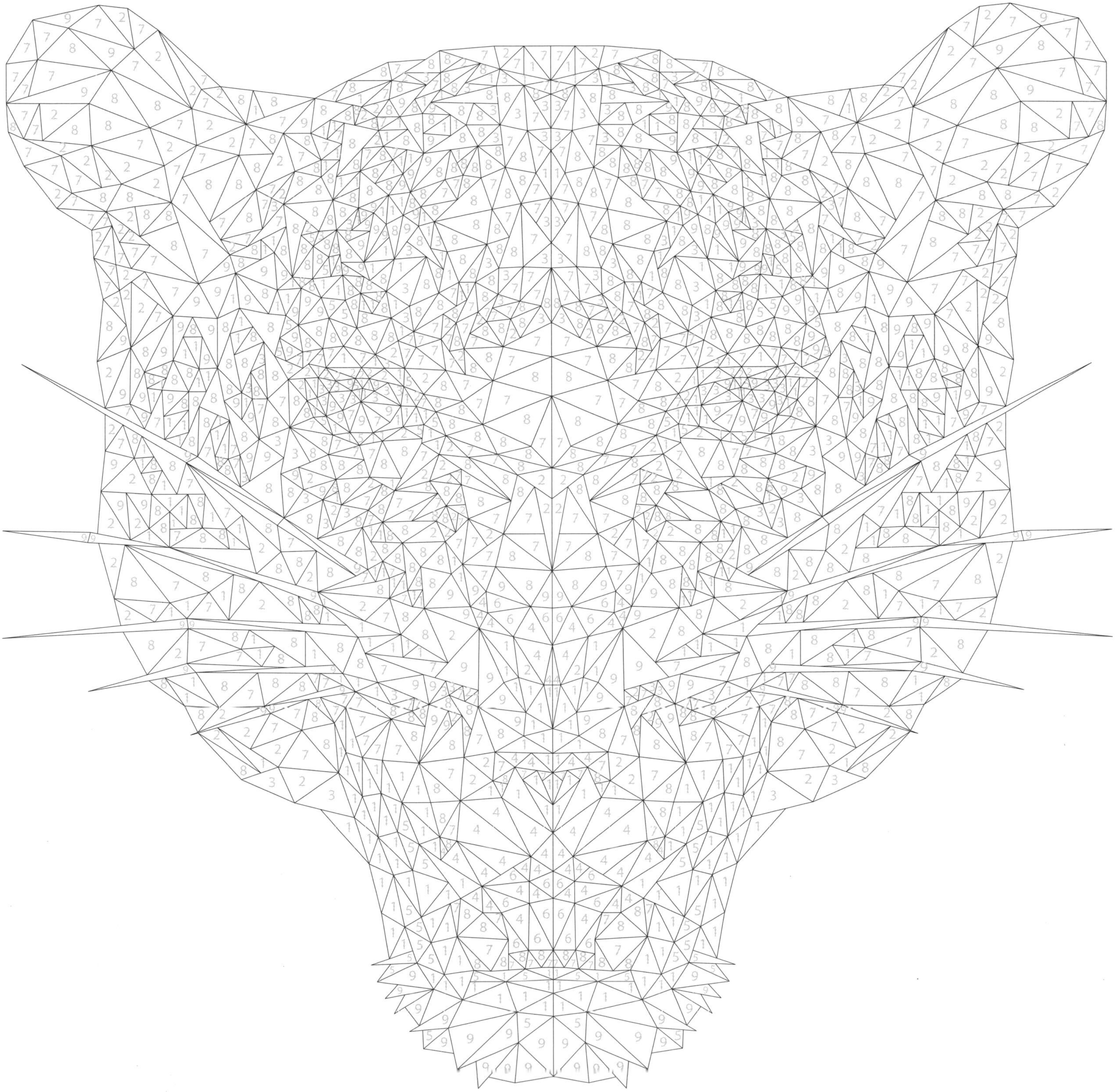

1 2 3 4 5 6 7 8 9

VIVID

# Tortoise

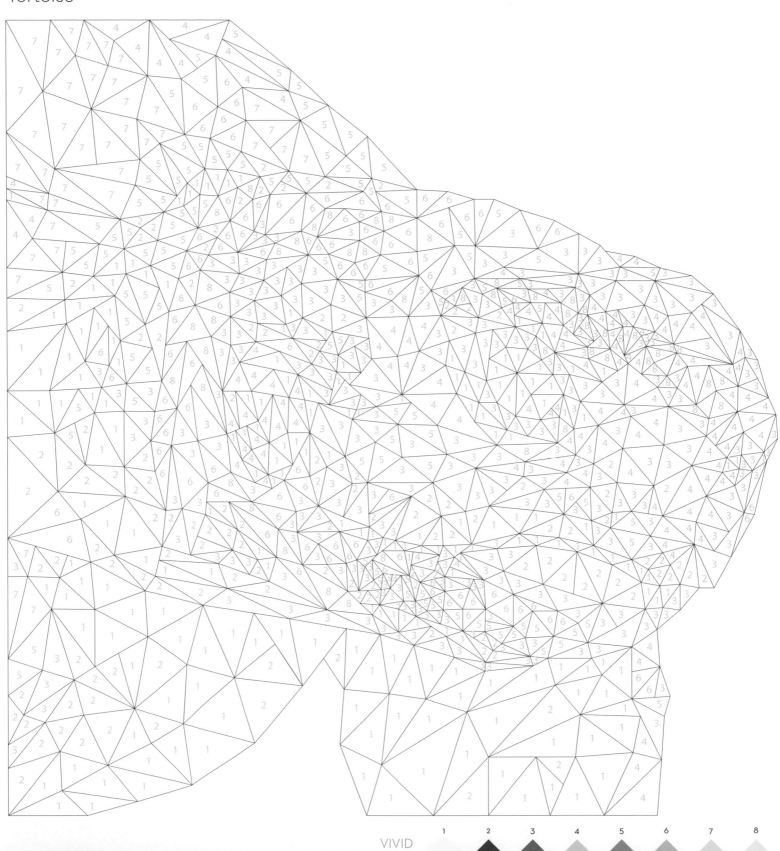

Opossum

# Brown Bear

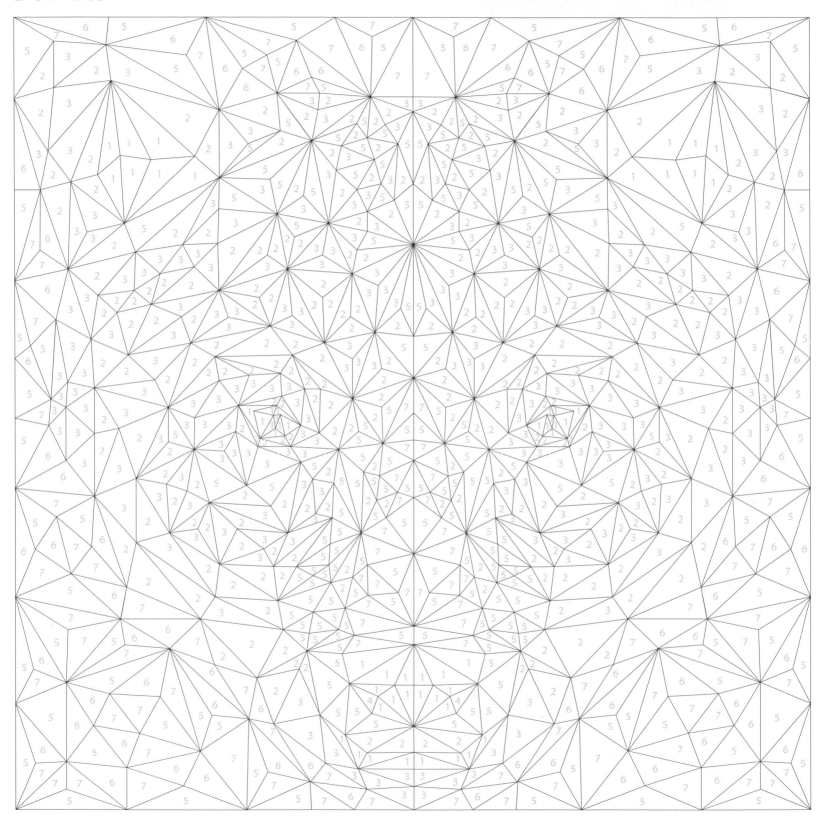

1  2  3  4  5  6  7  8  9

Golden Lion Tamarin

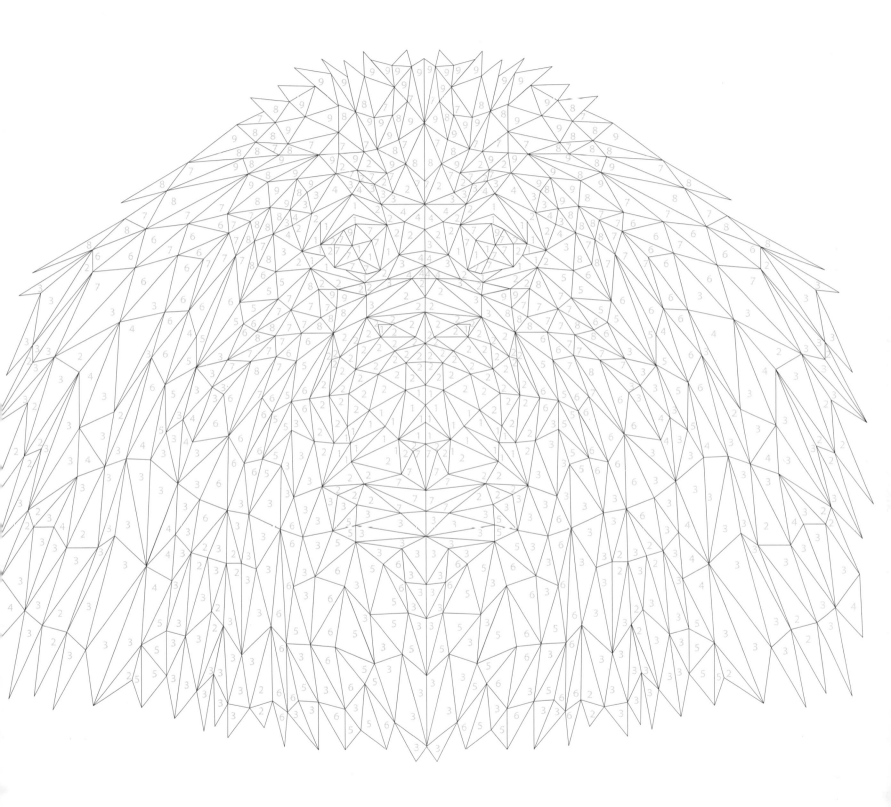

1  2  3  4  5  6  7  8  9

# Hyena

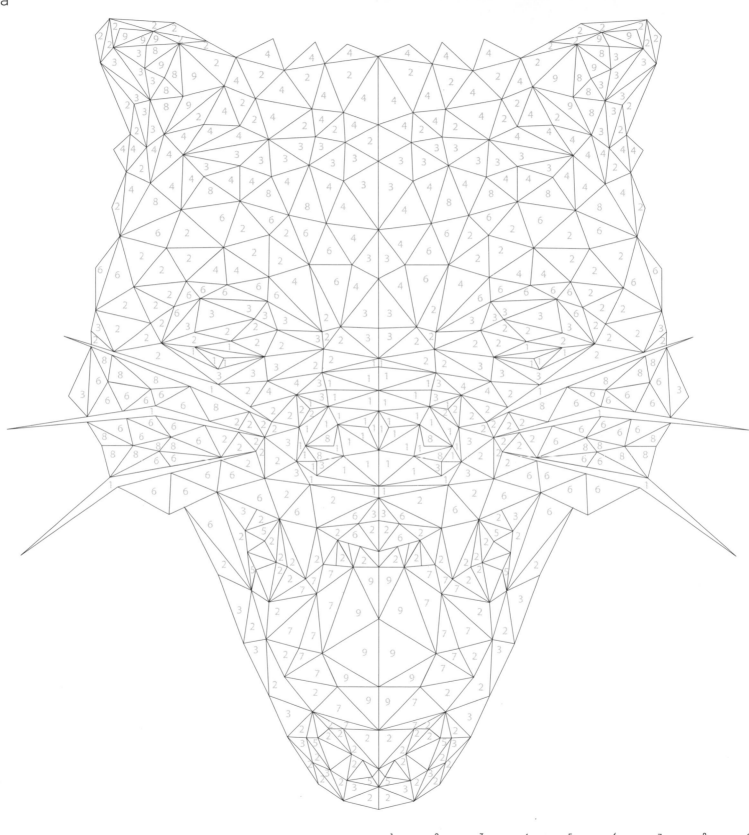

Mandrill

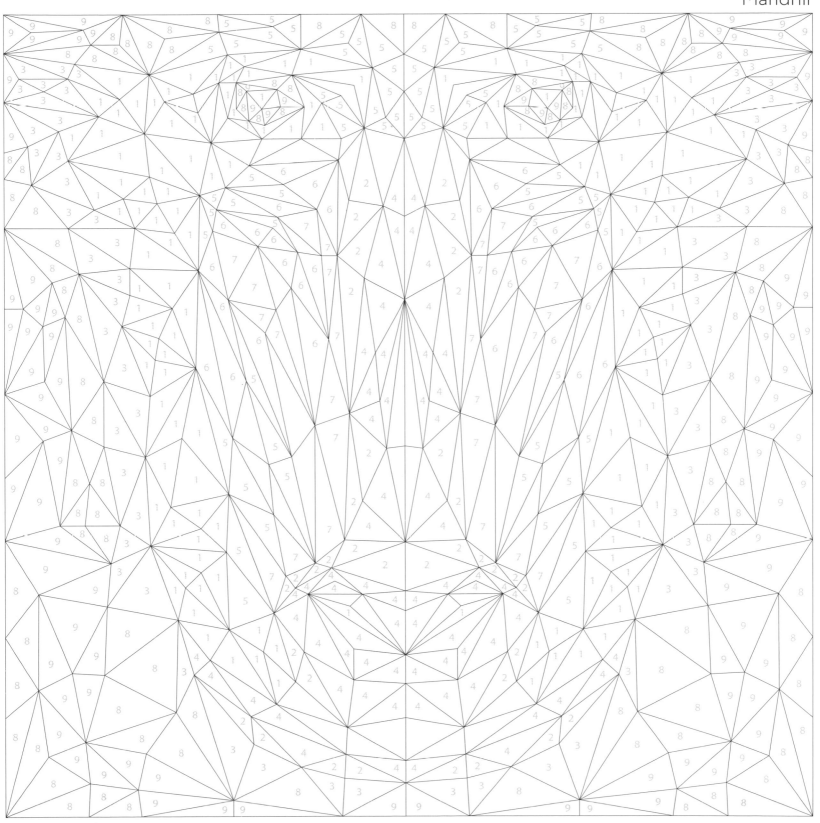

# Koala

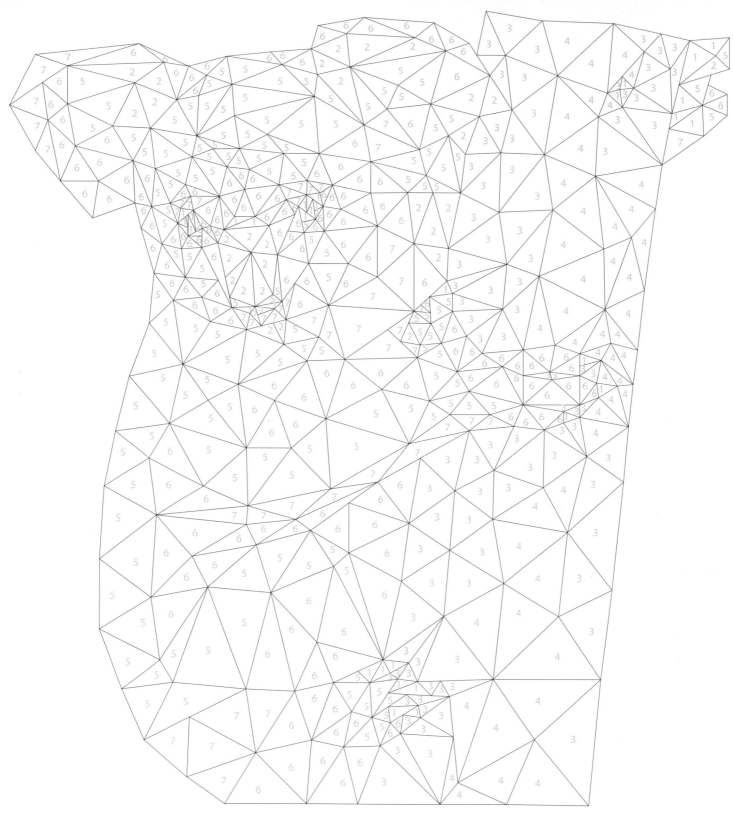

VIVID

Freestyle with your own colours

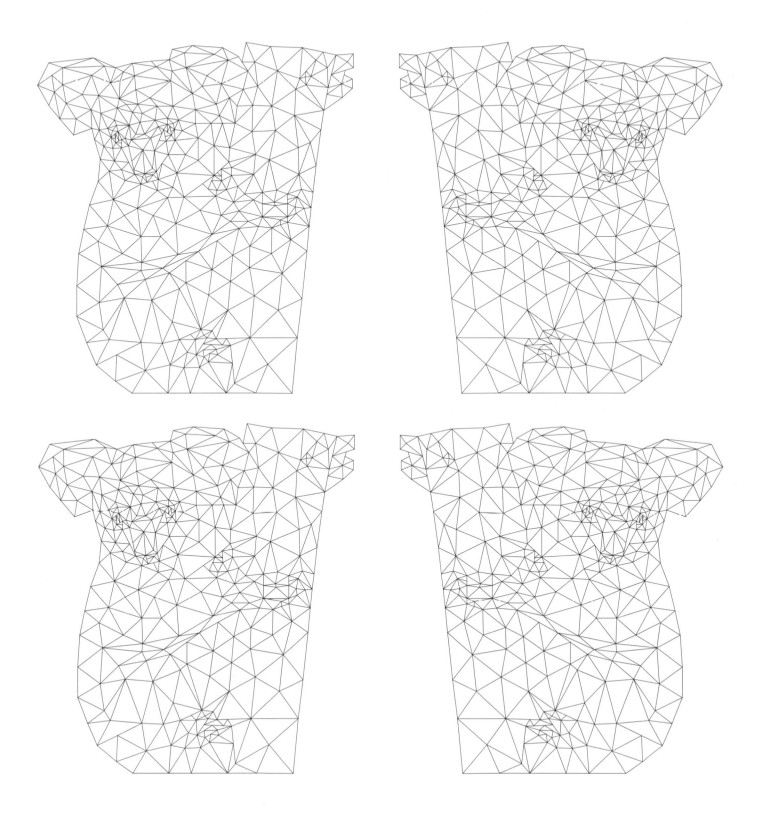

# Alligator

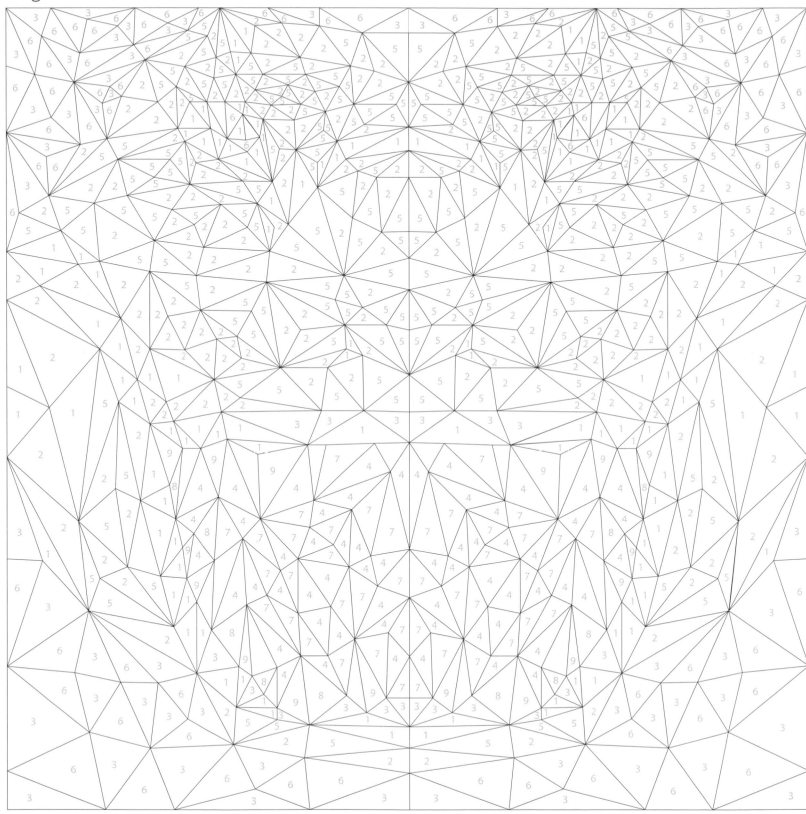

1 2 3 4 5 6 7 8 9

Fox

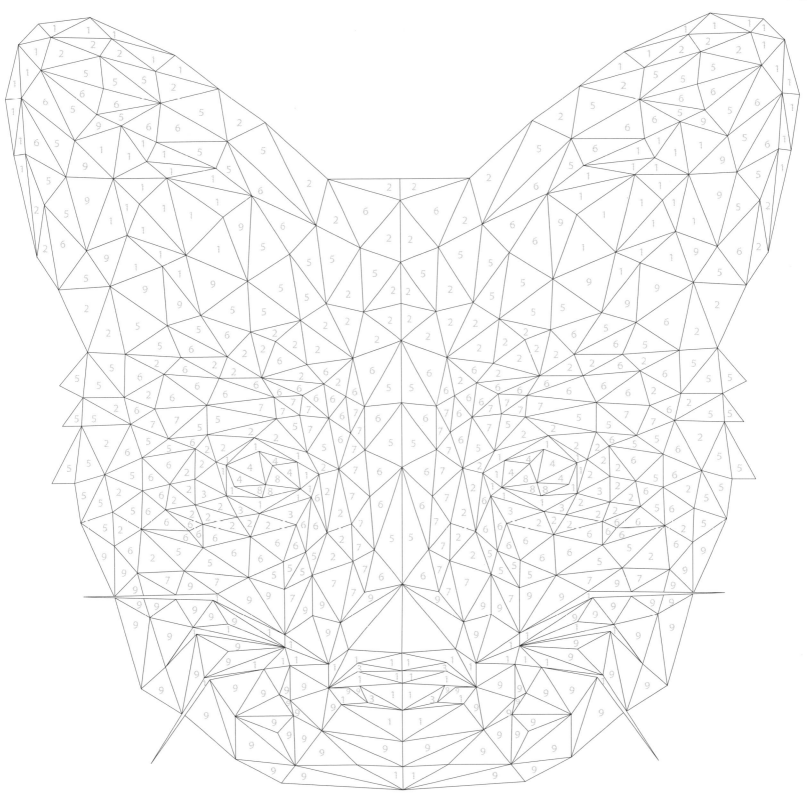

1 2 3 4 5 6 7 8 9

# Llama

Camel

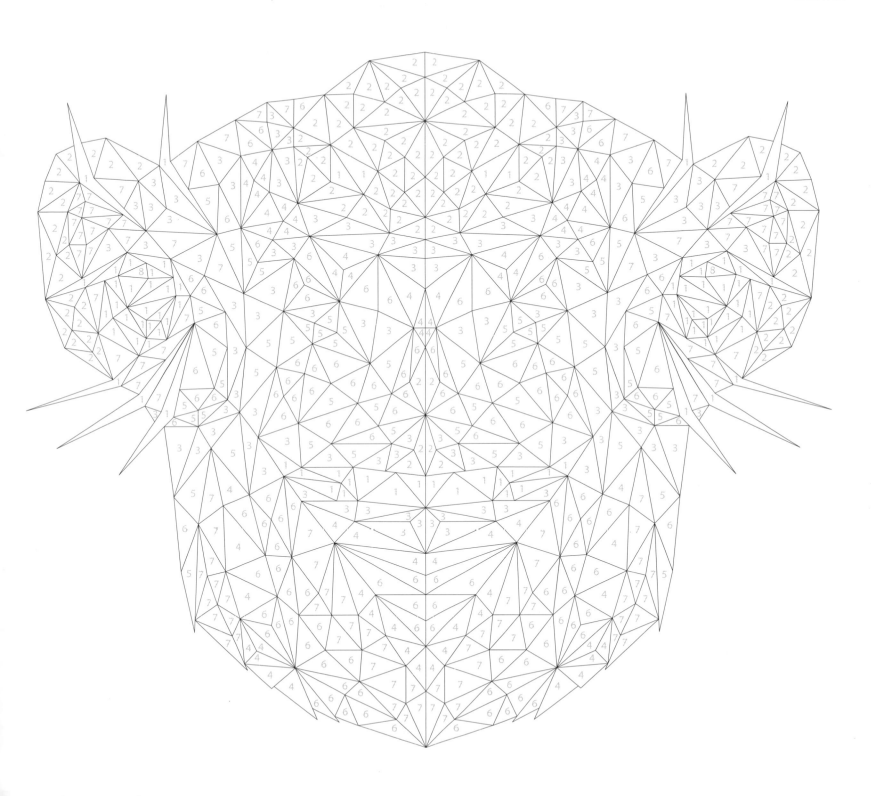

# Badger

1 2 3 4 5 6 7

Beaver

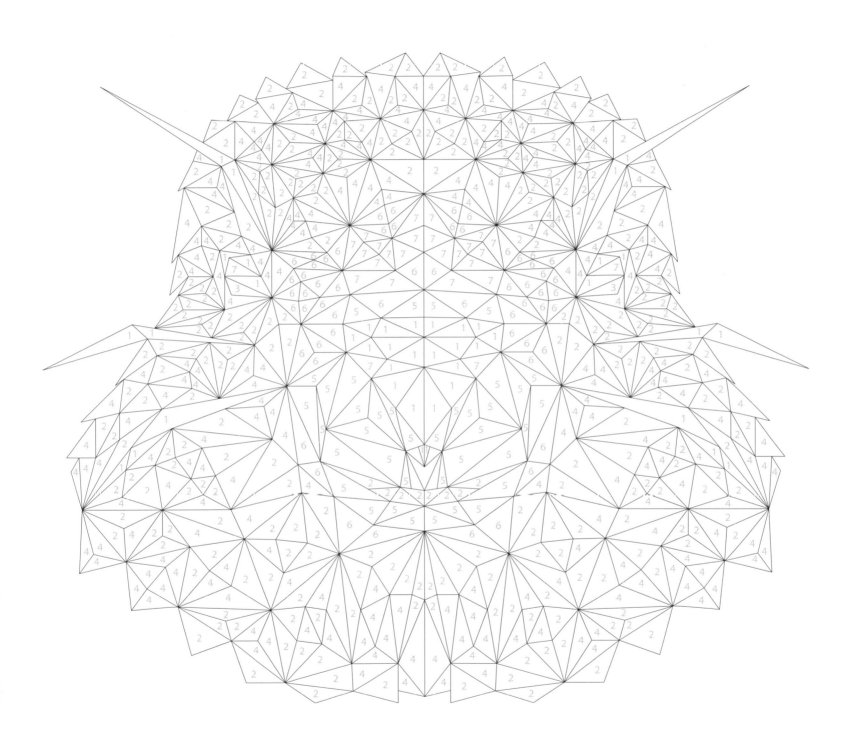

# Elephant

1  2  3  4  5  6  7  8

Kangaroo

1  2  3  4  5  6  7  8

# Red Squirrel

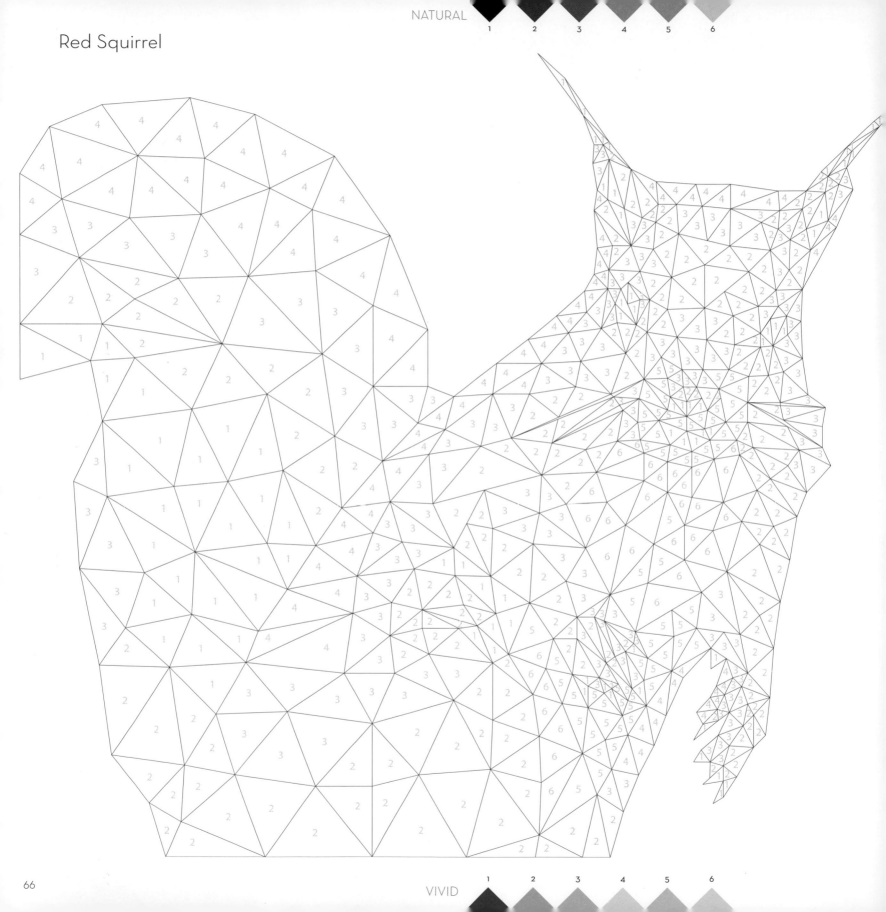

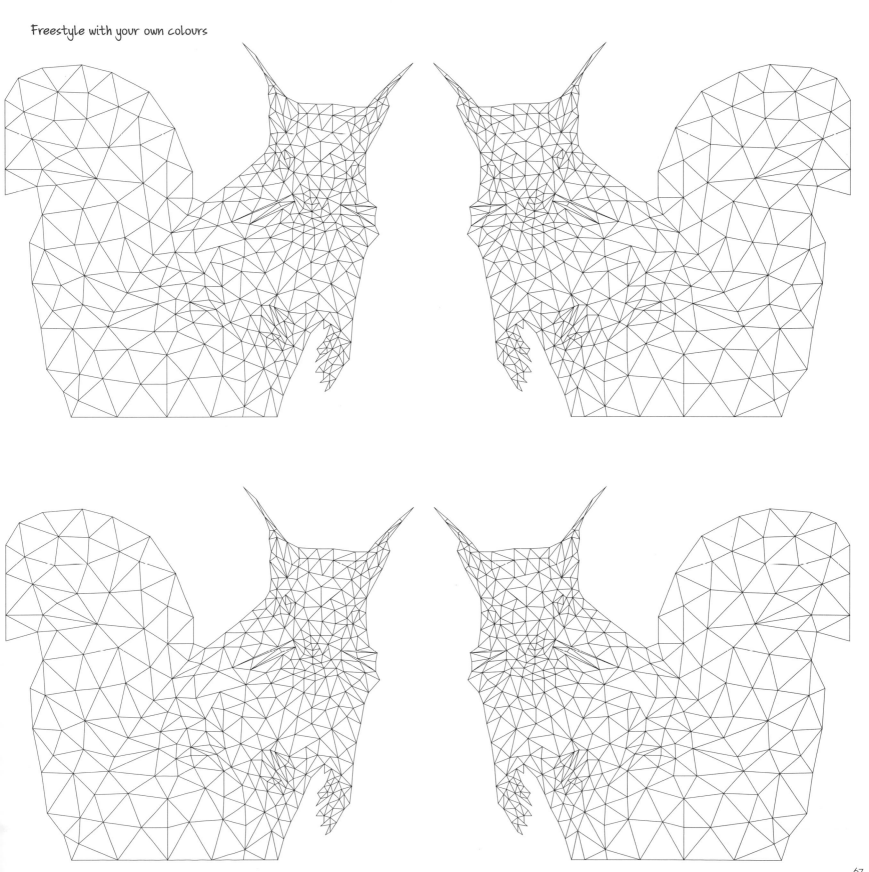

# Panda

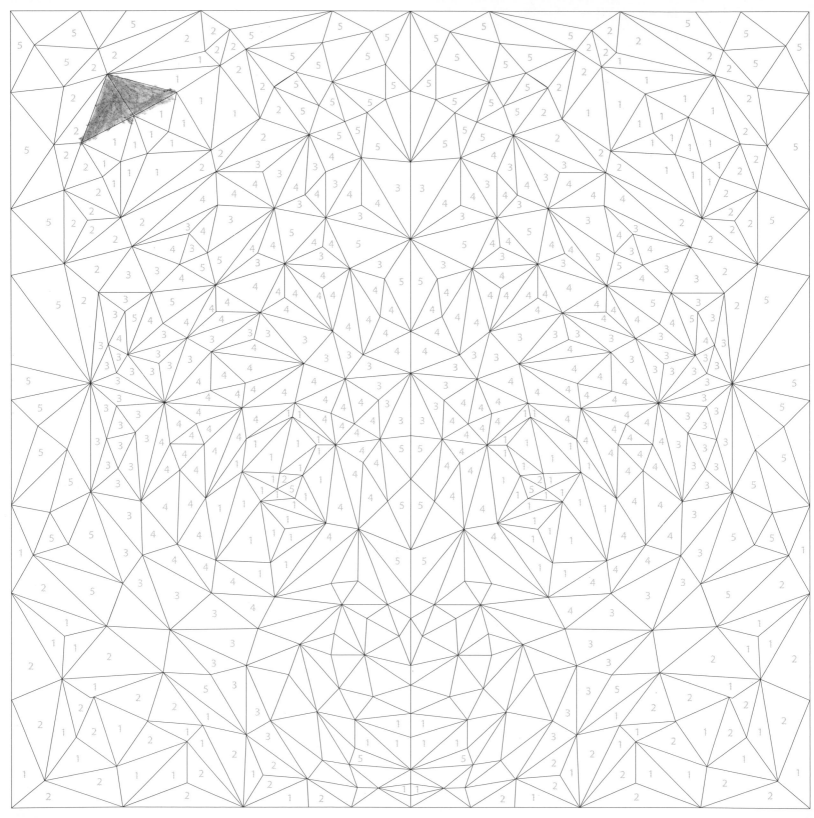

Wolf

# Lioness

Wombat

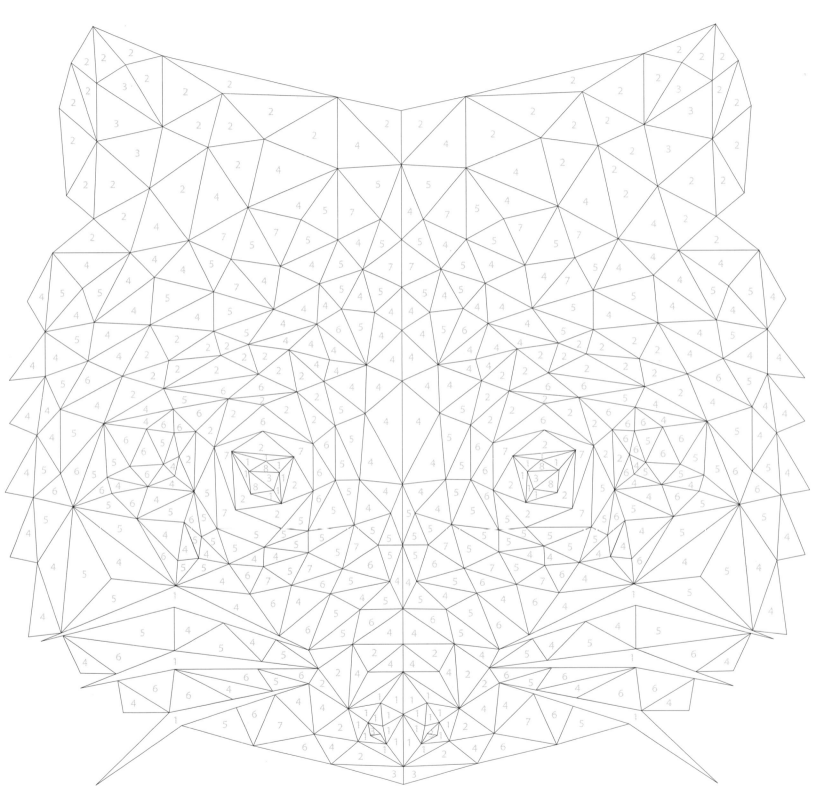

# Wild Boar

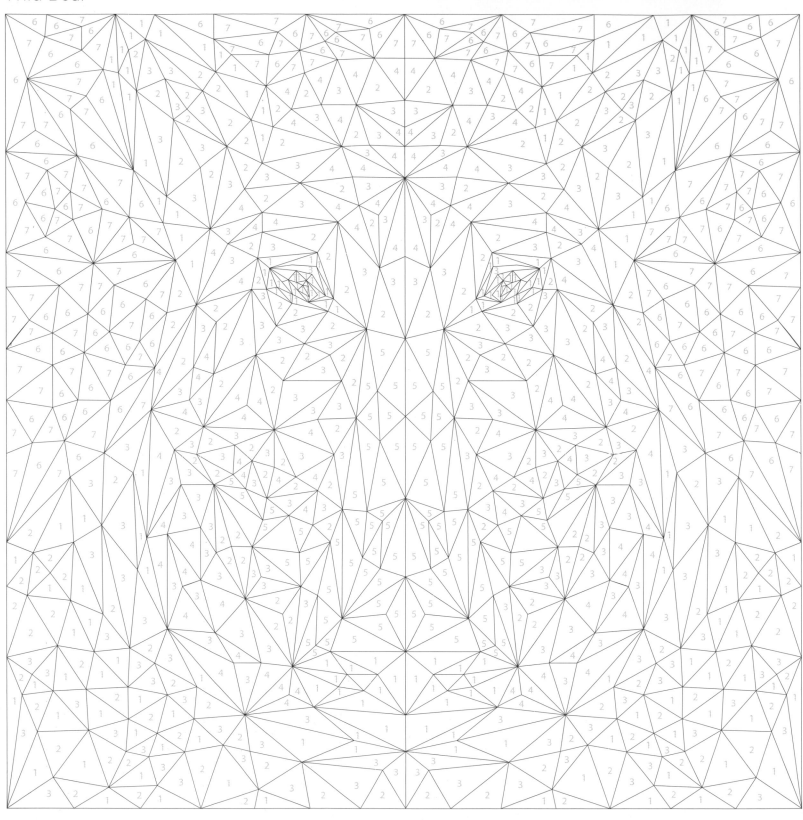

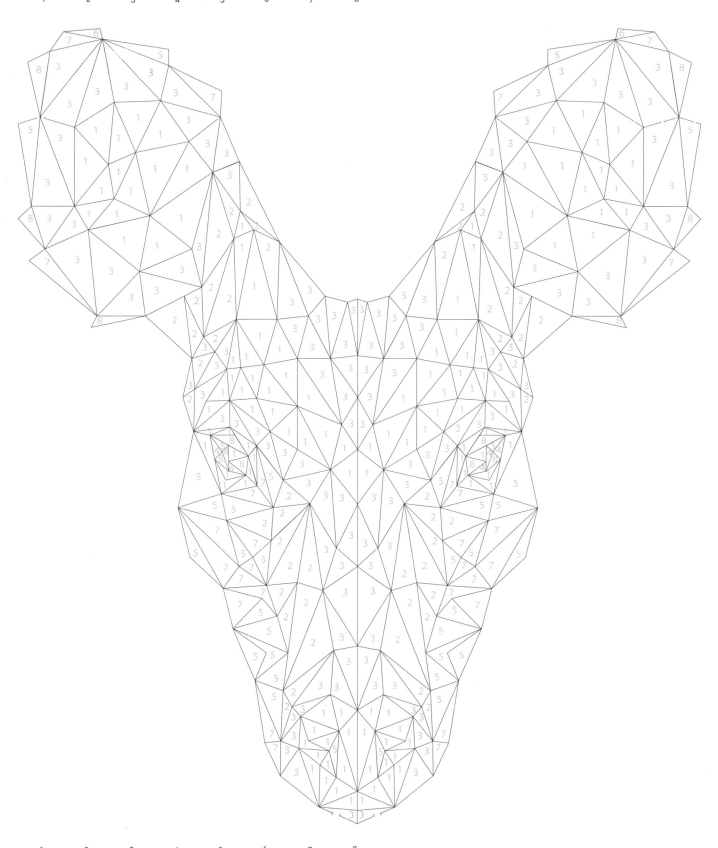

# Cape Buffalo

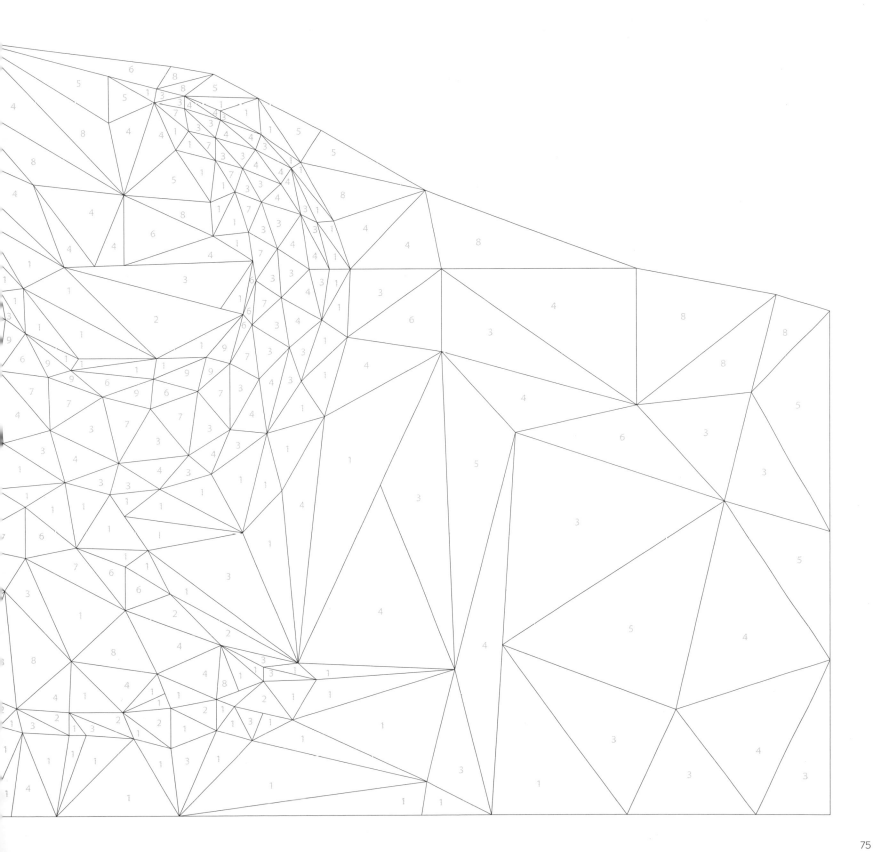

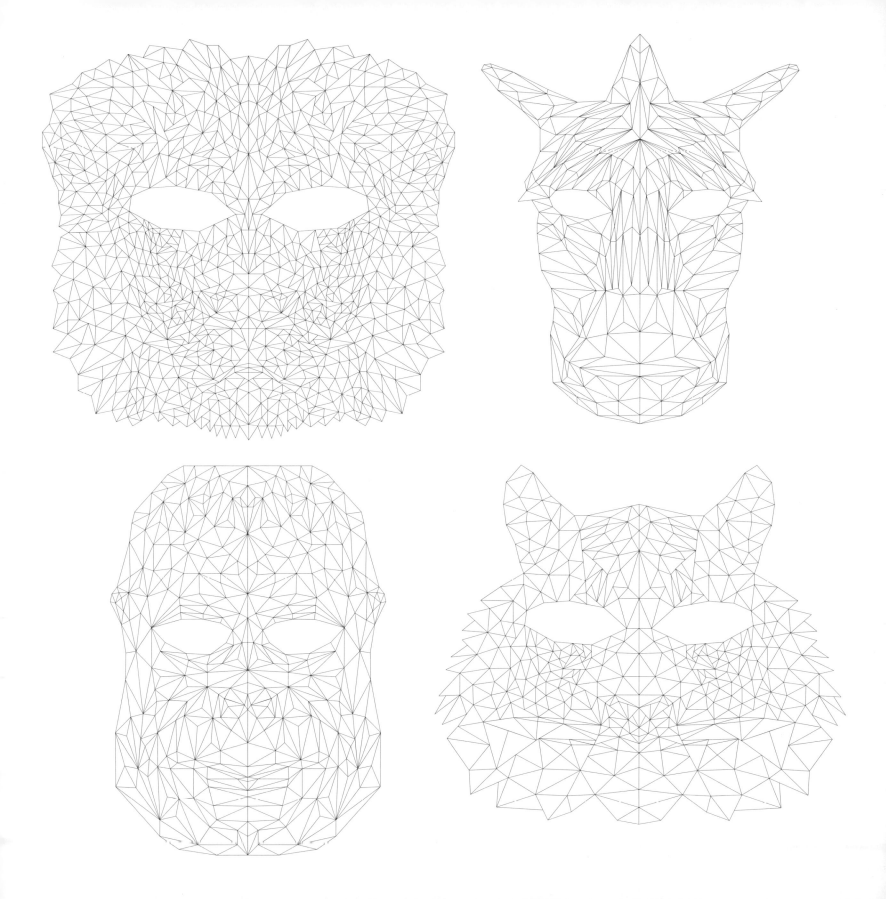

## HOW TO MAKE YOUR MASK

Once you have finished colouring your wild animals you may want to use them rather than keep them hidden away in the book. You could frame your finished images and create a whole wall of exotic creatures, adding colour to a dreary corner.

For a fun way to show off your works of art, you can also turn your animals into masks. With eight templates to choose from, including a zebra, tiger, owl and chimpanzee, there's something for everyone. You could do this as a group activity, maybe in your art class, or at work as part of a team-building session.

### TOP TIP

The faces are eye-catching enough, but if you want to make an animal mask that really grabs people's attention, you could try adding feathers, fur, gems, glitter or googly eyes. But don't overdo it, less is definitely more.

## CREATE YOUR MASK IN THREE EASY STEPS

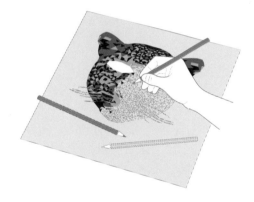

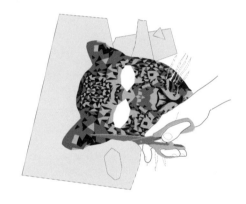

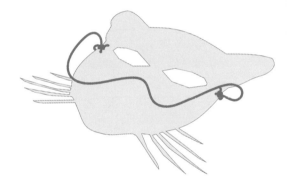

1) Colour in your chosen wild animal face using the natural or vivid palette.

2) Carefully tear your finished page out of the book – we've added perforated pages to make this easier. Use scissors or a craft knife to cut around the image and then cut out the two eye shapes. At this stage you may want to reinforce the paper with cardboard for extra stability, but this is not essential.

3) Use a piece of elastic that's suitable for tying at the back of your head to keep the mask in place. Make two small holes on either side of the mask; this is where you will attach the elastic. You can use hole reinforcement stickers (available at craft and stationery shops) so that the elastic doesn't tear your mask. Tie the elastic firmly in place on both sides of the mask. Now you are ready to show off your wild side.

Zebra

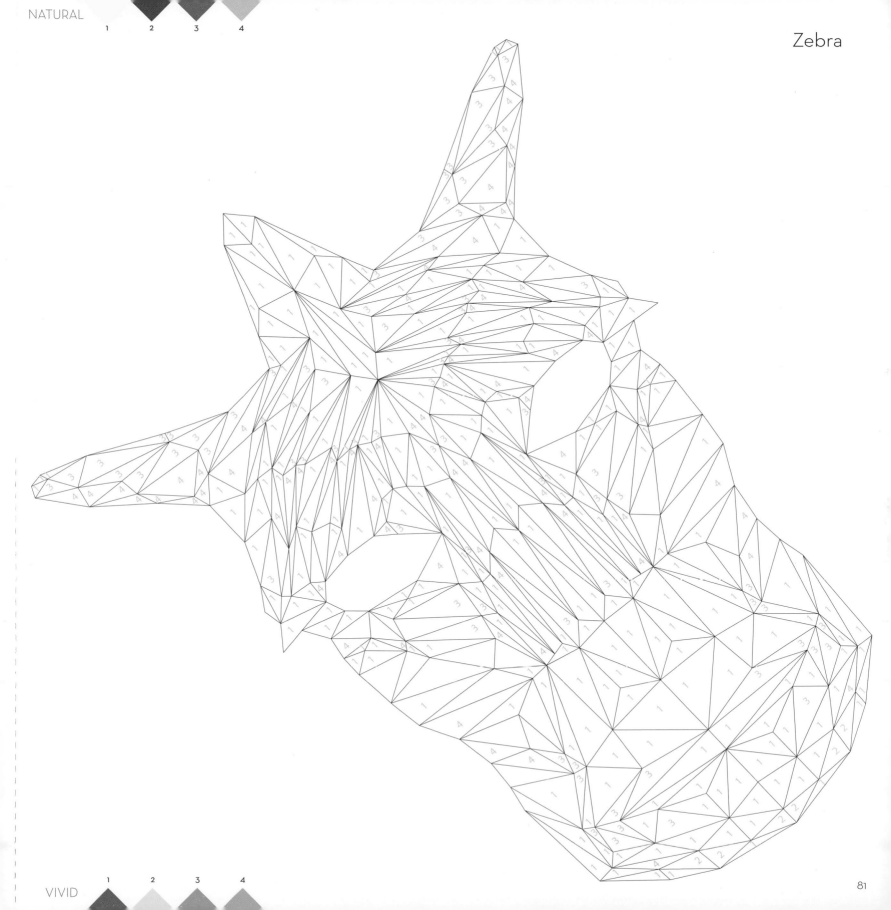

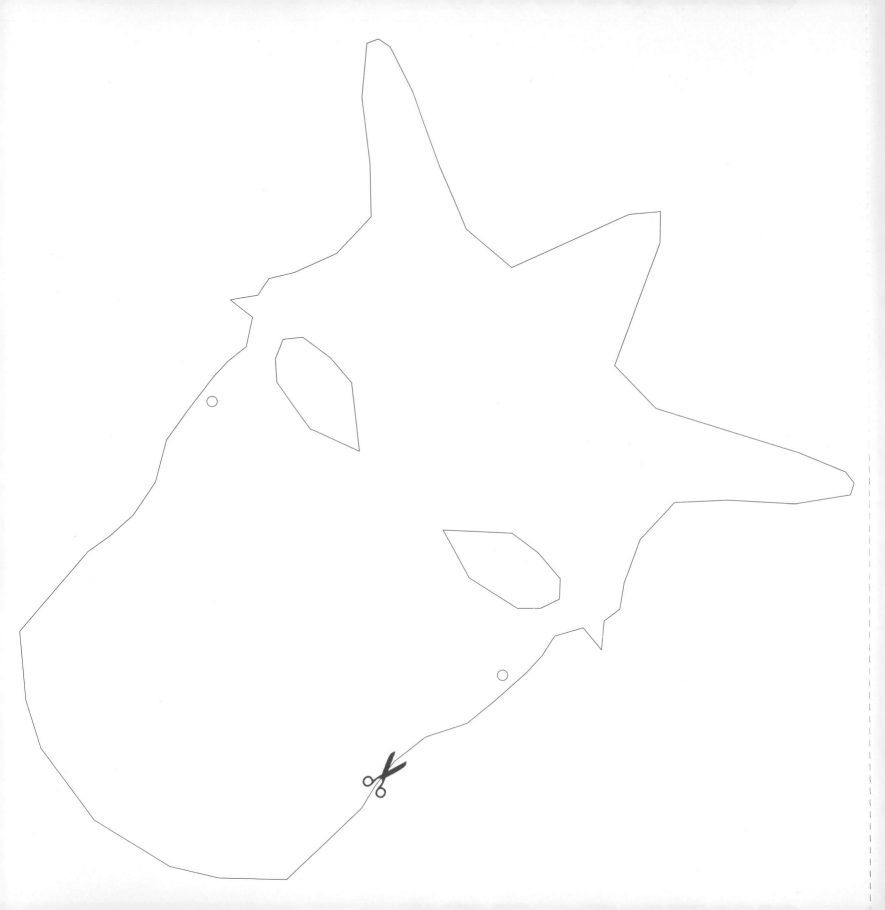

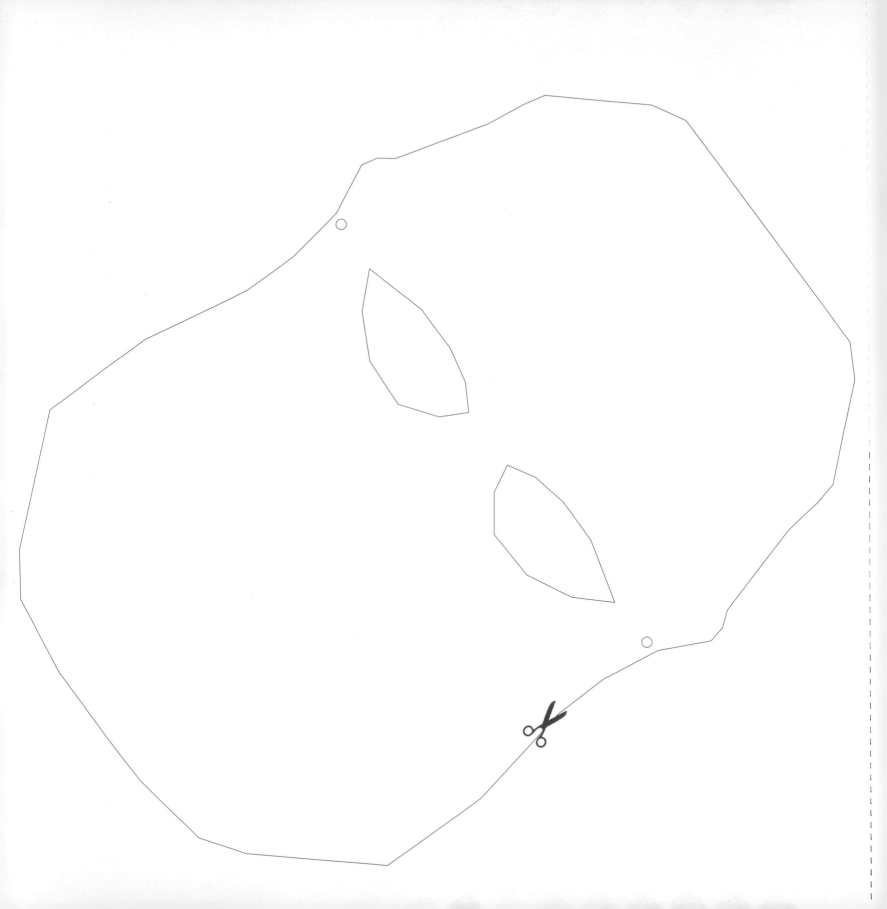

Tiger

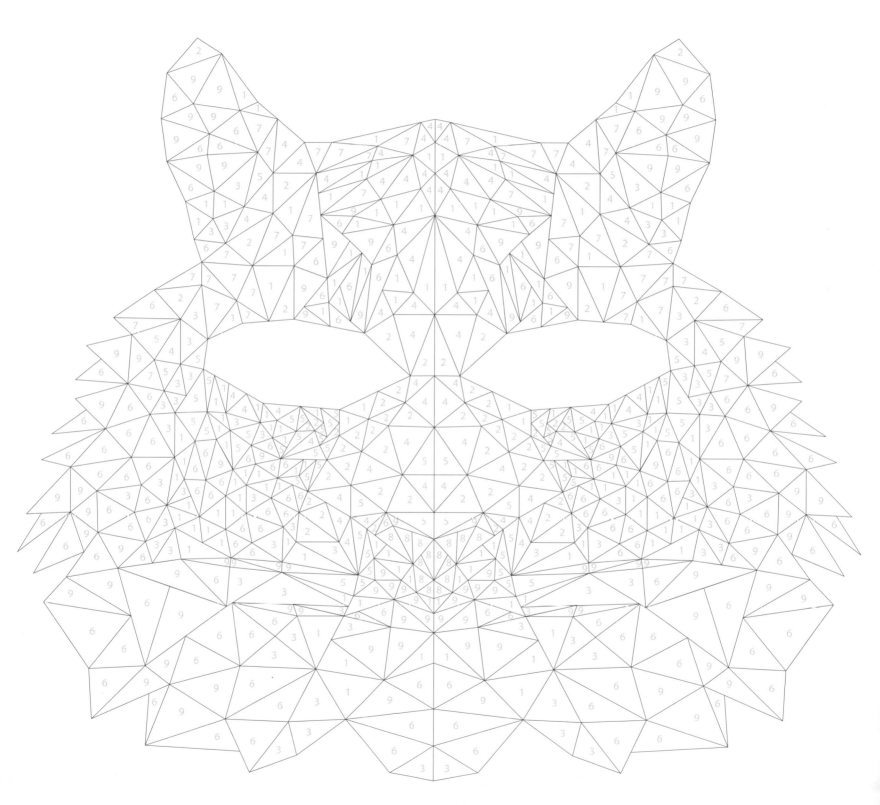

Vampire Bat

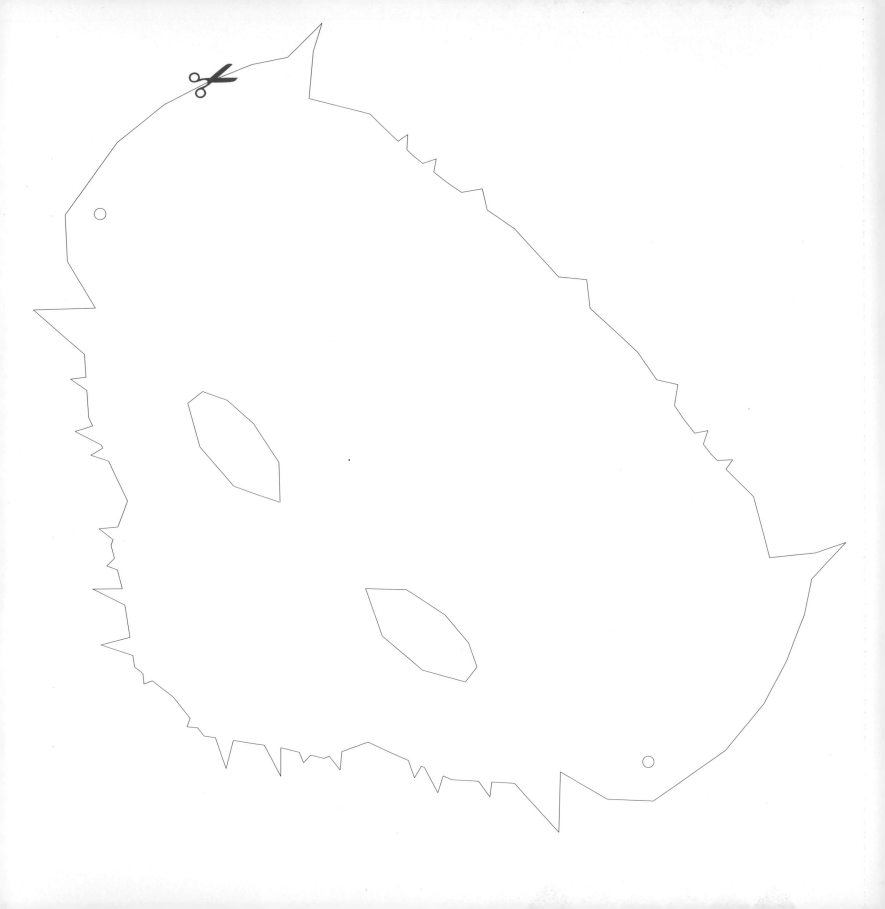

Lion

1 2 3 4 5 6 7 8 9

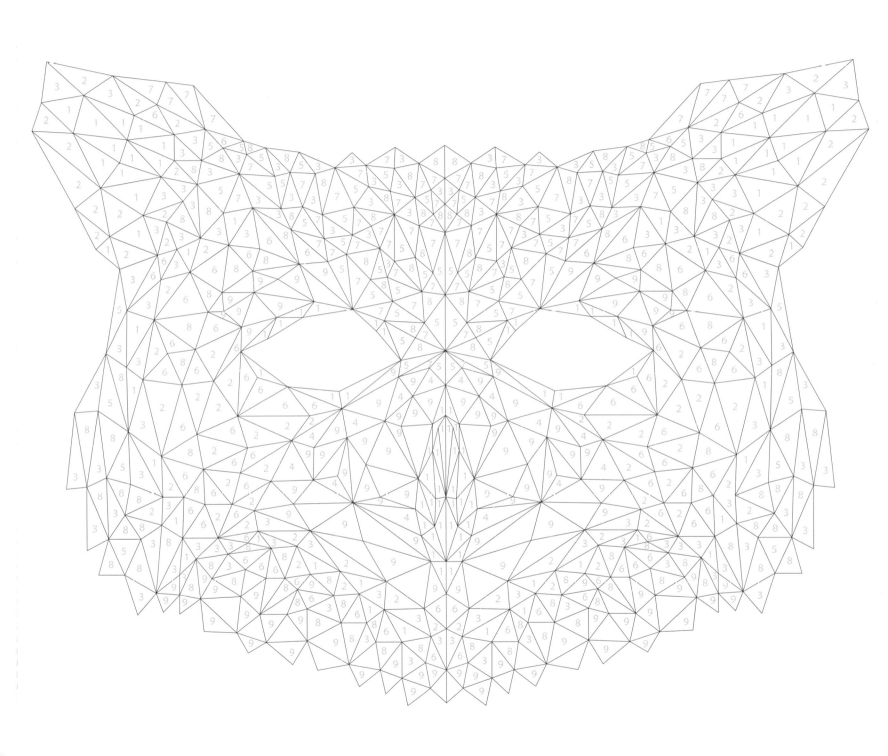

1   2   3   4   5   6   7

Leopard

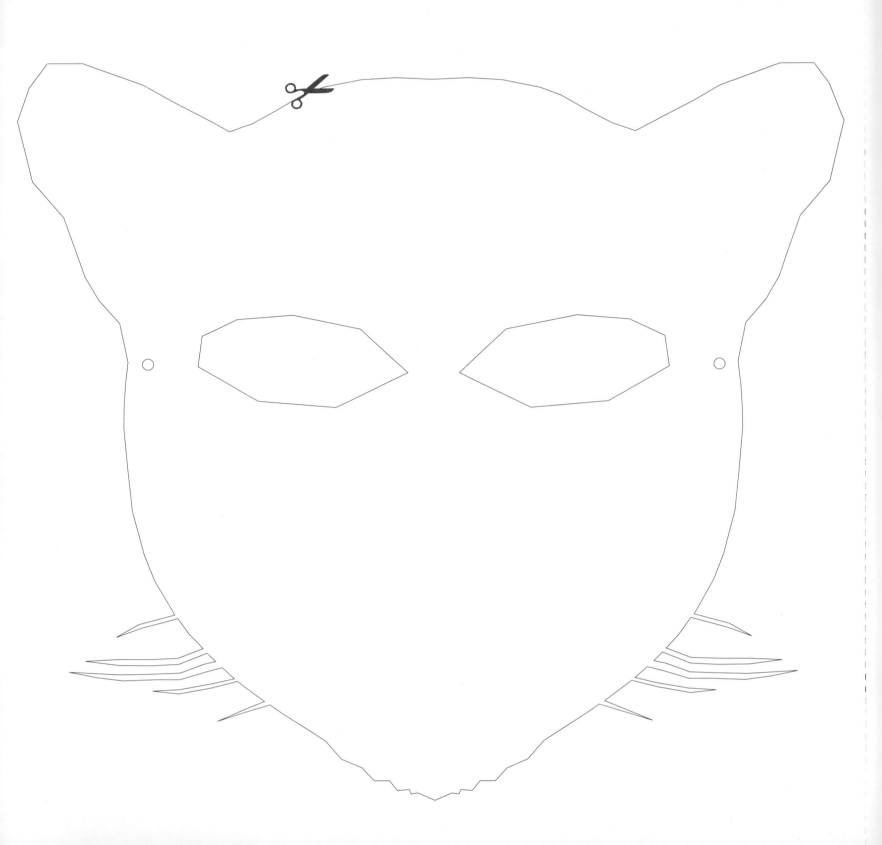

Chimpanzee